Making the Numbers Count

Making the Numbers Count

*The Accountant As Change Agent
on the World Class Team*

Brian H. Maskell

Publisher's Message by Norman Bodek

Productivity Press
Portland, Oregon

Productivity Press
P.O. Box 13390
Portland, OR 97213-0390
United States of America
Telephone: 503-235-0600
Telefax: 503-235-0909
E-mail: service@ppress.com

Cover and text design by William Stanton
Composition by Caroline Berg Kutil
Printed and bound by Edwards Brothers in the United States of America

Library of Congress Cataloging-in-Publication Data

Maskell, Brian H.
    Making the numbers count : the accountant as change agent on the world class team / Brian H. Maskell.
        p.   cm.
    Includes index.
    ISBN 1-56327-070-6
    1. Managerial accounting. 2. Accountants. 3. Industrial management.
    I. Title.
    HF5657.4.M375   1996
    658.15'11--dc20   96-15622
                                                            CIP

01 00 99 98 97 96   10 9 8 7 6 5 4 3 2 1

*For my family, Barbara, Caleb, and Sam, whose love and
support make all these endeavors possible.*

Contents

Publisher's Message

Performance measurement is the critical ingredient in successful continuous improvement programs. For many years Productivity Press has been publishing books saying that a revolution in management accounting is required to support the manufacturing process revolution initiated by the Toyota Production System of Ohno and Shingo. A recent customer survey indicated that many of our readers have established teamwork, employee involvement, and quality measurement programs, and have achieved some reduction of work-in-process inventories. Still it is clear that very few have fully implemented the essence of process improvement to become world class companies.

Brian Maskell has written about performance measurement and agile manufacturing in previous books published by Productivity Press. In *Making the Numbers Count* he challenges managers and accountants to reexamine the role of accountants in improving company performance. This book is his call to action. It's about placing the final, critical piece in the world class methodological puzzle, the piece that makes sense of the entire quality improvement picture.

Maskell begins this controversial book by examining the traditional role of accountants and then clarifying the role of a *proactive accountant*. Next he raises the primary issues of world class and agile manufacturing strategies and sets forth the challenge to simplify. The second half of the book summarizes the major tools accountants can use to transform their roles from passive financial recorders and reporters to active participants in value-added management to become leaders in the performance measurement revolution. He concludes with a strategy for implementation of this new approach to accounting.

At the end of *Making the Numbers Count*, the author presents an accounting and measurement diagnostic questionnaire. World class companies, those with fully evolved companywide process improvement and performance measures in place, will identify with the following statements:

- We run our business on primarily nonfinancial measures.
- We have eliminated cost accounting completely.
- We create only high-level budgets for planning purposes.
- We have worked hard to eliminate most of our accounting systems.
- Close partnerships with our customers, suppliers, and other third parties have enabled us to remove much of the traditional administrative waste.
- Our accounting people's primary focus is on process improvement and reengineering.
- Most of our accountants have now moved into operational areas where they spend most of their time on improvements projects—from operational improvement, to targets costs, to concurrent engineering, to marketing analysis.

If your company isn't doing all of this yet—whether you are a CEO, top or middle manager, or accountant—you need to read this book. At Productivity we have been adapting the principles of waste reduction to our own processes for many years. But, as in your companies, it has taken time to adopt the new accounting methods that will ensure full implementation of zero waste. With this book we are organizing a study group for our accountants and managers.

We strongly urge you to do the same. Maskell allows us no excuses. If having read his salient advice we fail to implement these methods, we can hardly complain when others who have taken up his challenge pass us by.

We wish to thank the author once again for choosing Productivity Press as his publisher. In addition, we wish here to acknowledge the many fine people who worked together to produce this book in record time: Diane Asay, editor-in-chief; Mary Junewick, project manager; Susan Swanson, production manager; Bill Stanton, text and cover designer; Caroline Berg Kutil for typesetting and Catchword, Inc. for the index.

Norman Bodek
Chairman and CEO

Preface

Working as I have with many manufacturing companies striving to achieve excellence, it has become apparent to me that accountants play a crucial role in any company. Sadly, in most companies accountants are a part of the problem and rarely a part of the solution. We speak much in the world class manufacturing movement about the elimination of waste in the processes; but the biggest waste I see is the waste of human talent, energy, and creativity throughout Western industry. Accountants are primarily bookkeepers and offer very little more to their companies; this is a tragic waste.

This book is not intended to provide a detailed explanation of new accounting methods; there are many other books that do so. It is intended to be a *call to arms* for accountants who want to stop "wasting" their time and begin to make an important contribution to their companies. All accounting tasks are non-value-added, but accountants can become highly value-added to their organizations if they can come out from under the ledgers and focus on change and improvement.

The working title for this book over the last two years had been the *Accountant as an Agent of Change*. Many of my colleagues were amused by this title, and made wisecracks about the traditional idea of accountants as dull and conservative people that would not recognize an innovation if they stumbled over it, let alone being able to initiate new thinking and change. Yet this is exactly the role accountants must actively seek if they are to be relevant to a company moving into world class and agile approaches to business.

Of all the business issues we face, accounting functions are the ones that can be most readily automated. The bookkeeping and primary report presentations are all regulated by law or by accepted practice, and all business software systems provide the ability to significantly automate these tasks. The accountant's first responsibility is to significantly reduce the amount of time and effort required to do the routine bookkeeping and reporting by eliminating much of the traditional accounting system as the company moves into world class status and gains greater control of its processes. He can also see to it that computer systems are used intelligently to eliminate the basic "grunt" work of posting transactions, handling payables and receivables, presenting the monthly books, and so forth.

Once his or her time is freed from the chains of the ledger and the computer screen, the accountant can begin the process of becoming a change agent. This is done through gaining a detailed and comprehensive understanding of the business, the products, the marketplace, and the myriad other activities of a modern manufacturing company. The job is then to work with others throughout the company to create change and improvement. Accountants must challenge themselves to come out of the cosy back room and become a street-fighter for change—to work with other people in the company to eliminate waste, improve processes, create partnerships with customers, suppliers, and other third parties, and develop a world class company that is capable of taking advantage of the turbulent and unpredictable times in which we work.

No book is a solo effort. The ideas and concepts presented throughout this book have been drawn from many sources and inspired by many people. I am indebted to my friend and colleague Bruce Baggaley (of Baggaley Consulting in Darien, CT) who has contributed a great deal to the ideas within this book, and has been an excellent sparring partner. I am also indebted to the many clients I have worked with over the years—too many to mention by name—who have striven to make excellence a reality in their organizations. It is easy and somewhat inspiring to create a vision for where a company should be going; but it is only by hard work, dedication, and excellence in the small things that visions can become realities.

These are challenging times for manufacturers, distributors, service companies, and every organization that is faced with the new competition of the global marketplace. This book is intended to inspire accountants within these companies to make a big contribution and help their companies become winners. If you would like to discuss these issues further, please feel free to contact me.

Brian H. Maskell
Voorhees, New Jersey

1

The Proactive
Accountant

Management accounting is a profession under fire. In the last few years a barrage of criticism has been leveled at the traditional techniques of management accounting, as well as at management accountants themselves. The fusillade has come from the accounting press, other trade and academic journals, and from people within manufacturing organizations. The author recently conducted a (very informal) survey in several American manufacturing companies.

The results were decidedly unflattering. It appears that management accountants are generally held in low regard by their colleagues and are not considered to be playing a useful role. The information they present is seen as wasteful, misleading, and causing more problems than it solves. Why is this?

The survey asked the following questions:

What word *best* describes the management accountants in your company?

What word *least* describes the management accountants in your company?

innovative	proactive	valuable	boring
tricky	progressive	isolated	dishonest
unhelpful	irrelevant	in touch	team member

The survey results were:

The words that *best* describe management accountants are boring, unhelpful, isolated. The words that *least* describe management accountants are innovative, proactive, progressive.

It used to be that companies were "run by the numbers"—many still are—that came from the management accounting department. It was generally accepted that managers needed this information to keep a finger on the pulse of the organization, to improve efficiencies, reduce inventory, and increase profitability. The monthly variance reports and budget analysis were the primary mechanisms for understanding the company's effectiveness. Capital investment projects lived or died on the assessment of the management accounting analysis of ROI and DCF. What are the reasons for this fall from grace?

Manufacturing in the Nineties

The world of manufacturing has changed beyond recognition in the last ten or fifteen years. Foreign competitors attacked Western markets in the late 1970s and decimated whole industries. They stole our markets by being better. American and European manufacturers recognized that they had to change, change fast, and change radically.

In the early 1980s quality became the issue. The better Japanese manufacturers could make products of significantly higher quality than we could. Western companies began to learn their "secrets": statistical process control to reduce variation, quality at source instead of inspection, design for manufacture, certified suppliers delivering on time with zero defects. The quality revolution hit hard. There are no quick fixes to create quality overnight. It takes a long-term commitment and an attention to detail that are foreign to most organizations. (Quality, just-in-time, and other world class methods are discussed in more detail in Chapter 3.)

The new competitors were also more nimble. They could introduce new products faster, were more responsive to the customer's needs, and had shorter lead times and much lower costs. In response, Western manufacturers began to introduce just-in-time manufacturing techniques: short cycle times, small batches, changeovers of less than 10 minutes, cellular manufacturing, synchronized production flow, kanban, and low, low inventories. These approaches broke all the rules.

The need to slim down overheads led to cataclysmic organizational changes. Autocracy and bureaucracy were replaced by the team approach and employee involvement. Responsibility was shifted to the sharp end of the business: the shopfloor, the warehouse, and the office. A work environment was created where everyone was responsible for their own quality, their own schedules, continuous improvement, and customer service.

Parallel with these changes was an increasing understanding that traditional costing methods were no longer relevant. The patterns of product costs had changed over the years as technology, production methods, and the market had changed. Studies showed that the standard product costs generated by the cost accountants were misleading and wrong. There were fundamental flaws in the tried and true accounting practices. (The problems caused by traditional accounting methods are discussed more fully in Chapter 2.)

What was happening to the management accounting department during this maelstrom of change? *Nothing.* The same systems, the same methods, the same approaches. The *real* issues of manufacturing became quality, on-time delivery, continuous improvement, customer service, time-to-market, and employee involvement. Management accounting did not address these issues.

Criticism of Management Accountants

A company moving into a teamwork approach cannot have a parochial and isolated management accounting group. Everybody else in the organization is getting cross-trained, is committed to quality and continuous improvement, and is on a team—or several teams. The barriers must be broken down, the departmental silos eliminated; the entire organization must work together to achieve common objectives. The management accountants—along with the industrial engineers, the designers, the quality people, the maintenance men, and other support groups—must become part of the team.

The introduction of world class manufacturing requires the elimination of complex and wasteful systems. Some of the most complex and wasteful systems in many companies are in management accounting. These include budgeting, inventory valuation, labor reporting, and the entire cost accounting system. Many of the traditional management accounting methods are not only wasteful but positively harmful to the organization. Management accountants must become proactive about simplification. This requires the elimination of most of the systems that are near and dear to us, that have been our bread and butter since we left college. (Chapter 4 provides a step-by-step approach to simplifying accounting systems.)

The accounting department is frequently accused of holding back progress to world class manufacturing. This is often true. Accountants tend to be conservative. Our training has given us a bias towards an arms-length approach to others in the organization. Our adherence to "generally accepted accounting practice" has led to a lack of imagination and innovation. We must reverse this and become innovative leaders in our companies, applying our analytical skills and financial savvy to creating a world class company. This will require a significant change of role for the management accountant. But it opens up important new opportunities. These opportunities require learning new skills, working in teams, and even folding the management accounting department into other company support areas. These changes are not easy to make—but they are essential.

The Proactive Accountant

The author has observed that the attitude of management accountants in companies implementing world class manufacturing varies considerably from one organization to the next. In some companies they are "on the team"—the accounting people are leaders in the quest for perfection. In other companies the accountants actively oppose change. The people who are bent on innovation and improvement must fight the accountants either by working around them or by the fine art of Machiavellian politicking. In most companies the accountants carry on "doing their own thing" despite the revolution taking place around their ears.

If you accept the assertion that all companies must improve radically if they are to remain competitive in the "white knuckle nineties," then you must recognize that radical change is needed in the accounting department. The management accountant must become proactive. He or she must become a leader for change and accept the change of role this requires.

This challenge is not unique to accountants. Radical change is taking place in all departments of the company. The introduction of just-in-time manufacturing on the shop floor is changing the lives of operators and supervisors alike. Concurrent engineering is making the job of the design engineer, industrial engineer, and quality worker totally different. The trend towards a customer-focused organization is changing the role of marketing, sales, and customer support personnel. Everyone's job is changing dramatically—management accountants are not exempt.

In recent years the move towards world class manufacturing has been driven primarily by quality assurance staff, production managers, and (sometimes) product designers. The accountants and other support staff have tended to stand by and watch—or hold back progress. This is no longer the case. In many world class companies the management accountants are becoming proactive leaders creating excellence not only in their own areas of responsibility but also across the entire company.

Attributes of a World Class Management Accountant

Flexibility is an underlying theme of world class manufacturing. The management accountant must become flexible in his or her approach. First the accountant must become a team player. There is no room for the old isolation of the accounting office. The accountant will find himself on the shop floor working with the quality team, in the design office working on concurrent engineering, or working with marketing on customer service issues. These groups will often be self-directed work teams that have no manager or supervisor; the accountant is just one of the team.

Coupled with the change to teamwork is an enthusiasm for diverse activities. New vistas of opportunity and challenge are open to proactive accountants. The old cost accounting days are now long gone. The accountant is participating in the full gamut of business activities: new product planning, marketing, customer service, production, quality, continuous improvement, as well as financially driven projects.

A keystone of world class manufacturing is a bias towards simplicity. Management accountants, and Western industry in general, have in the past had a proclivity to complexity. The operations research mentality used to prevail—if you have a complex problem, find a complex method of analyzing and solving the problem. World class manufacturers take the opposite view. If you have a complex problem, simplify it. It is easy to invent complicated solutions, but it requires skill and ingenuity to simplify the problem. Management accountants need to recognize that their role is to simplify problems and eliminate complex systems, including the accounting systems.

An important aspect of simplicity is a willingness to abandon traditional approaches. The spurious argument given time and again by reluctant accountants is that they must adhere to general accepted accounting practice (GAAP). This *is true* of financial accounting because the government has a bad habit of putting financial accountants in jail if they violate accounting practice. But the internal control of an organization is entirely under the control of the company itself. The accounting methods used must support the company's world class objectives. This means that the accounting systems must become the servants of production, marketing, and engineering —not the other way round.

These kinds of changes cannot be made in a vacuum. Another attribute of a proactive accountant is a willingness to learn. So much is changing in modern manufacturing. Some of these changes are technical, some of them—the more far reaching ones—are philosophical. It is important to be a learner.

What has been discussed in the preceeding paragraphs is a revolution in thinking and practice for the average management accountant. We need to take these revolutionary steps if our companies are to be competitive in the global market of the 1990s.

Tools and Techniques

As we move our analytical skills into new areas of the production organization and abandon many of the traditional methods, there are new techniques we must learn. The first approach is very general. The average management accountant is woefully ignorant of the company's processes and procedures. Many do not have a clear understanding of the accounting and administration procedures because these tend to be complex and convoluted. Very few have more than a passing knowledge of the manufacturing processes, not to mention the engineering and technology the product uses. To be a valuable contributor to your organization you must be intimately familiar with the company's products, processes, markets, and customers. You must also have a clear understanding of what people in other departments think, feel, and do. These things are not learned in training classes. They are learned by taking the time and effort—often in your own time—to get alongside other people in your organization and become a part of the team.

In addition, there are many tools and techniques that *can* be learned in the classroom. This list is not exhaustive. It is intended to show the diversity of activities a world class management accountant can participate in. In later chapters we will look at these methods in some detail.

- *Activity-based costing*
  Accounting technique designed to assign more accurate product costs by understanding the activities that create cost and allocating overheads based on those activities.

- *Activity-based management*
  Using the understanding gained from studying cost-creating activities for process improvement and increased effectiveness.

- *Customer profitability*
  Understanding and analyzing cost and profitability of customers and distribution channels, and from the ultimate customer's perspective.

- *Performance measurement*
  Abandonment of traditional, financial performance measures and developing performance measures that are congruent with the company's world class goals.

- *Value-added analysis*
  Understanding the company's production, distribution, and support processes with a view to identifying what adds value and what does not. This is a powerful tool for improvement and for measurement.

- *Process mapping*
  Graphical, team-based method of analyzing a process to create improvement.

- *Target costing*
  Technique for matching planned product costs with market value of the product during the design phase of the product's life.

- *Value engineering*
  Formal process for matching the product features at the lowest possible cost.

- *Variety effectiveness process*
  Systematic approach to reducing cost and complexity through standardization of components and production process, while providing customers with a wide choice.

- *Life cycle costing*
  Analysis of product costs and profitability across the entire life of the product or product family. A long-term view from our perspective and that of the customer.

- *Quality function deployment*
  Formal method for matching customer needs and expectations through product design and competitive analysis.

- *Competitive benchmarking*
  Working with excellent companies to understand their reasons for success, and applying these success factors in your own company.

The Role of the Management Accountant

The role of the management accountant changes radically in a world class manufacturing environment. The accountant becomes useful. This is a paradigm change. Management accounting in traditional organizations is very much a non-value-added overhead. The accountant gathers data, creates reports, uncovers variances, analyzes projects, and creates budgets. None of these activities create improvement; indeed the process is wasteful, confusing, and impedes the progress of a company striving to become a world class competitor.

Toshiro Hiromoto, the Japanese pundit, wrote "one of the areas I believe contributes mightily to Japanese competitiveness is how many companies' management accounting systems reinforce top-to-bottom committment to process and product innovation." (Hiromoto 1988). Many studies of Japanese management accounting methods have concluded that Japanese management accounting methods are similar to those of Western companies. Nothing could be further from the truth. They are so different that Western "experts" cannot recognize the differences. The fundamental role of accountants in the better Japanese companies is to create improvement and cost reduction, very often during the product design process at the source of cost. Many of the accounting *methods* are similar to those of the West; the *concepts* of accounting are fundamentally different.

The new role for management accountants is to line themselves up with the world class goals of the organization, become part of the team, and help the company move ahead. This requires flexibility, a willingness to change, and a desire to become involved in the real issues facing the organization. This new role can be uncomfortable, but it is also challenging and rewarding.

These are some of the activities in which an accountant will participate:

- *Manufacturing*
  - ▶ Total quality management teams seeking to perfect the process and eliminate production variation.
  - ▶ Just-in-time implementation. Working with shopfloor personnel, industrial engineers, and others to eliminate inventory, increase cycle times, and implement cellular manufacturing, total productive maintenance, and so on.

- *Purchasing*
  - ▶ Supplier reduction, long-term supplier relationships, supplier certification, and target costing of purchased items and materials.

- *Product development*
  - ▶ Part of a concurrent engineering team using target costing, value engineering, life cycle costing, QFD, and other world class methods.

- *Marketing*
  - ▶ Product costing, market driven pricing, target costing of customer service activities, customer and product profitability.

- *Waste elimination*
  ▶ Value-added analysis, activity-based management, lead time reduction, and continuous improvement.

- *Performance measurement*
  ▶ Development of nonfinancial, focused performance measurement system in line with the company's strategic direction.

- *Accounting simplification*
  ▶ Systematic elimination of complex and wasteful cost accounting, variance reporting, budgeting, and inventory control procedures.

- *Human resources*
  ▶ Working with cross-functional teams to create a gainsharing system that is in line with the company's world class goals.
  ▶ Participating in the total employee involvement programs.

Summary

Most of what a traditional management accountant does is irrelevant, wasteful, and potentially harmful to a world class company. There is a vital new role for management accountants who are prepared to become proactive contributors to the company's world class goals.

A world class management accountant must be:

- Flexible
- A team member
- Willing to participate in diverse improvement activities
- Biased towards simplicity
- Willing to abandon traditional methods
- Aware of the need for education and training

Questions

1. Why are traditional management accountants regarded as irrelevant and wasteful by world class manufacturing people?

2. How can the management accountant become a proactive part of the world class team?

3. What are the attributes of a world class management accountant?

4. List some of the techniques a management accountant should add to his or her toolbox.

5. What kinds of projects and teams can benefit from the participation of a proactive management accountant?

2

Shortcomings of Traditional Accounting Methods†

Professors Kaplan and Johnson, authors of the influential book *Relevance Lost: The Rise and Fall of Management Accounting*, have stated that "cost accounting is the number one enemy of productivity." (Kaplan and Johnson 1987). Strong words. There are three principle shortcomings of traditional accounting systems: they are irrelevant and harmful to the business, they are expensive to maintain, and they divert the accountant's attention from more important matters. The average accountant in an American manufacturing company spends up to 75 percent of his or her time on bookkeeping activities and less than 10 percent on analysis and process improvement. The job has been reduced to a backward-looking, reactive recording and dissemination of data that, if it could be done by a machine, would make the accountant entirely unnecessary.

---

† This chapter and the next provide background information about traditional accounting methods and the concepts of world class and agile manufacturing. Readers who are anxious to move into the practical application of the issues raised in Chapter 1 may want to skip ahead to Chapter 4 that deals with accounting simplification.

We must distinguish between financial accounting and management accounting. Financial accounting is the task of preparing and presenting an accurate representation of the company's business to outsiders, principally the SEC, the shareholders, and government agencies like the Internal Revenue Service. This process is highly regulated and it is important that the information (balance sheets, P&L, and so forth) be accurate and presented according to the regulated standards. The government feels so strongly about this that they put you in jail if you violate the standards. Cost and management accounting, on the other hand, is used internally to help the company's managers control and improve the business. While there are accounting standards associated with these tasks, there is no legal requirement to perform these tasks in any particular way or to perform them at all. A company can do as much or as little cost and management accounting as it wishes, and it can do these things any way they want. Cost and management accounting are for internal use and must be of value to running the company's business.

As with any non-value-added but required task, it is important that the financial accounting processes be stripped down to their bare requirements and automated as much as possible. All non-value-added activities must be either eliminated or simplified so they take the minimum amount of work, effort, and time. Fortunately these things are among the easiest of business functions to computerize because they are regulated so strictly. The objective of an accountant in a company moving towards world class is to use the computer systems to eliminate the bulk of the regular financial accounting and bookkeeping activities (including accounts payable and receivable) so that their time can be spent on the more important issues of analysis and business improvement. (For more detail, see Chapter 4.)

In most companies the financial accounting systems, manual and automatic, are much too complicated and time-consuming. They include numerous manual journal entries, complex accruals and allocations, lengthy matching of invoices with purchase orders, and so forth. The month-end procedures are conducted with Byzantine complexity and the final reports are often produced manually using home-grown spreadsheets that are pored over for many hours and days, instead of being printed directly from the primary computer system. Many of these reports, particularly those concerning budgets and variances, result in lengthy, time-wasting, useless meetings that deal more with assigning blame than creating improvement. This is not only wasteful in itself, but it also diverts attention from the real issues of moving the company towards world class stardards.

Cost and management accounting is intended to help companies control and improve their business. Unfortunately the traditional approaches to cost and management accounting fall down badly as a company moves away from traditional approaches and into world class methods. The time-honored cost and management accounting methods were developed in the late nineteenth century and early twentieth century to meet the dynamic needs of expanding industries in Europe and the United States. The concepts were formalized by the 1930s and have since been the basis for manufacturing financial control. However, in the last 15 or 20 years profound changes have taken place in Western manufacturing industry, but the techniques and concepts of management accounting remain unchanged.

History of Management Accounting

The historical development of management accounting is fascinating. Contrary to the popular myth depicting accountants as humorless men in gray suits, the people who were responsible for introducing the concepts of cost accounting were dynamic and innovative leaders. These business people were among the pioneers of the nineteenth-century industrial explosion.

Although the principles of financial accounting and bookkeeping were developed in the fourteenth century as a method of tracking commercial endeavors, management accounting was not required by the merchants and small business owners of the years prior to the industrial revolution. It was the advent of large industrial organizations in the nineteenth century that created a need for information about the financial transactions occurring within these companies.

New accounting methods were developed because entrepreneurs were beginning to hire people on a long-term basis, make long-range capital investments, establish hierarchical company structures, and introduce more complex production technologies. The new decision making within these enterprises required new internal financial information systems.

Early costing systems concentrated on conversion costs for the calculation of cost-per-ton and cost-per-unit of straightforward manufacturing processes like steel making. These costs included labor and materials, and occasionally the application of a little overhead. As communication and transportation improved during the nineteenth century, new management techniques were required to control more far-flung enterprises like railroads, retail stores, and services. These needs brought the development of cost and profit centers, and new performance measures for individual branches.

The influence of the scientific management movement, with its emphasis on a standard method for each production task, led to the introduction of standard costs for manufactured products. The diversified corporations that began to develop in the early twentieth century required the use of budgeting, capital investment analysis, performance measurement ratios, and divisionalized accounting.

All the essential elements of modern management accounting had been established and codified by 1930. These elements included financial forecasting, budgeting, standard costing, overhead absorption, variance analysis, transfer pricing, return-on-investment calculations (ROI), and so forth. In addition, the integration of the cost accounts with the financial accounts had by that time become accepted practice and was required by the auditors. At the same time business schools and professional institutions were formed and began to teach "modern" business methods. The techniques of management accounting became established practice.

Since the 1930s there have not been any significant changes in the techniques of management accounting. Many refinements have been introduced, a great deal of academic work has been done, but the fundamental principles have not changed. In contrast to this stable picture, manufacturing industry has changed enormously. Products have changed dramatically. Production technology has been transformed and automation has changed cost distributions. Research and development cycles in some industries are much longer and more costly, and employee needs and aspirations are very different. In short, a revolution has taken place in industry and the rate of change is increasing every year. Traditional methods of management accounting have not kept pace with these dynamic changes.

Problems with Management Accounting

The problems with management accounting fall under five major headings:

1. Lack of relevance
2. Cost distortion
3. Inflexibility
4. Incompatibility with world class approaches
5. Inappropriate links to financial accounts

1. Lack of Relevance

- *Management accounting reports are not directly related to the company's strategy*

  Management accounting systems are, by their nature, primarily financial in the way they collect and report information. But the strategic goals of world class companies are primarily nonfinancial. The strategic goals will often make reference to financial objectives—and these goals can generally be reported through the *financial* accounting system—but most of the goals are nonfinancial. These include such issues as products, markets, quality, reliability, flexibility, innovation, time-to-market, lead times, customer satisfaction, employee involvement, and social issues. None of these issues are addressed by traditional management accounting. If management accounting does not address the strategic issues of the company then it is, by definition, irrelevant.

- *Financial measures are not meaningful for the control of production and distribution operations.*

  Most people in a factory do not think in terms of the financial aspects of their work; they concentrate on such issues as production rates, yield, quantities, on-time deliveries, reject rates, schedule changes, and stock-outs. These are the real issues of manufacturing; not contrived financial analogs.

  Do the managers or supervisors in your plant get excited when they hear the management accountant is bringing their monthly variance reports? Do they exclaim: "Wow!! These reports are really going to help us improve the process and do our jobs better." Of course they don't. Why not? Because the management accounting reports provide nothing of use or value to anyone in the business operations. In fact, they know that the results shown in the reports are going to cause them a problem because they will have to go to lengthy and useless cost variance meetings where they will have to "explain" why the costs are different from standard or some other fiction.

- *The application of cost accounting to pricing is often misleading and irrelevant.*

  Management accounting analysis has become less significant to pricing decisions in recent years because world-wide competition has made product pricing market-driven and not cost-driven. Few companies have the luxury of setting their own prices according to an acceptable margin above the product costs. Those days are largely gone.

  Consequently there is now significant change in the way products are marketed. Many companies are much more concerned about market share and long-term viability than about the markup on an individual product. This change, among others, has led to significant competitive pressure for Western manufacturers. The new requirement is to set the price according to the needs of the market to give the company a competitive edge, and account must be taken not only of that product but also of other aspects relating to customer service, additional value-added services, and the long-term relationship with the customer.

For the majority of manufacturers (other than some defense suppliers) prices are established by marketing decision rather than by analysis of costs. There is still a need to analyze production costs in comparison to prices so that managers can understand product, customer, and channel profitability. The requirement is to match costs to the market price and the required profitability; and to view this over the longer term profitability of the product or the family of products. The techniques of target costing, life cycle costing, and value analysis are the accounting tools required in this environment (see Chapter 8, *Product Design*), and not the traditional product cost and profitability analysis.

2. Cost Distortion

• *Traditional cost accounting is concerned with cost elements. The pattern of cost elements has changed in recent years and this detailed analysis is less important.*

Back in the days when cost accounting was developed, the breakdown of costs into cost elements was quite straightforward. Labor was by far the biggest cost element for most products, materials coming next, and overheads were relatively small. This is no longer the case. The average American manufactured product receives less than 7 percent of the total cost from labor, and overheads are a huge contribution to cost The traditional methods of breaking down product costs into elements is (at best) irrelevant and often harmfully misleading.

- *The distinction between direct and indirect costs is not as rigid as it used to be. The same is true of fixed and variable costs.*

Once again, in the early days of cost accounting there was a clear distinction between direct and indirect costs. Direct costs were costs directly associated with making the product and indirect costs were other company activities that contributed cost but did not contribute to making the product. These included overhead activities like management, product design, sales and marketing, and so forth. Those indirect costs were relatively low in comparison to direct costs. Today this is no longer the case and the ideas associated with direct and indirect costs do not apply.

Many world class companies are emphasizing teamwork, continuous improvement, and employee empowerment. These approaches require the previously *direct* employee to become involved in many activities that were previously done only by *indirect* people. These include scheduling, process improvement, problem solving, interaction with customers and suppliers, and sometimes hiring and firing. These changes blur the traditional distinction between direct and indirect employees, and render the concept unhelpful in analyzing and understanding costs.

Similarly, the use of fixed and variable overhead costs is not as clear-cut as it used to be. There are some overhead costs that are fixed (the president's airplane, for example) and have no relationship to the products being manufactured. Other overhead costs are indeed variable according to product and quantities being manufactured. But the majority of overhead costs have no clear-cut fixed/variable characteristics. The use of electricity, for example, may be variable in one part of the plant and fixed in another. This distinction is unhelpful in analyzing and understanding product costs and how to improve the company's operations.

- *Traditional methods of apportioning overheads can significantly distort product costs.*

This is the problem of allocating overhead costs using labor hours or labor costs. In the early days overhead amounts were small and labor hours and costs were high; it made good sense to apply the overhead costs according to labor hours or costs. These days labor costs are low and overhead costs are high and companies that continue to apply overheads using labor as the driver are misleading themselves, often with very serious consequences. It is not uncommon for a company to close down a product line because it is "unprofitable" only to find that their idea of profitability was flawed because overheads were erroneously applied.

The issue goes deeper than just saying that overheads applied using labor hours or costs can distort the company's product costs. The real issue is how can overheads be "correctly" applied to product costs? Some companies take the approach that the application of overheads to products is always misleading and make their management decisions based on marginal and direct costs only. Other companies have adopted the ideas of *activity-based costing* where the activities associated with the development, production, and distribution of the products are analyzed and each activity is costed. (See Chapter 5.) The product costs are determined by applying these activity-based costs according to the amount of use each product makes of each of the activities. This provides a more appropriate understanding of product costs, but does require a considerable amount of analysis work to be done.

3. Inflexibility

- *Traditional management accounting reports do not vary from plant to plant within an organization. Similarly, they do not change over time as the business needs change.*

One of the charms of traditional management account-ing is that the reports are consistent across the company, the divisions, and the entire corporation. A single set of numbers controls the whole organization. While this has aesthetic merit it does not make sense for a world class organization. An important aspect in the implementa-tion of world class methods is that each site or each plant is different. They have different products, different processes, different strengths and weaknesses, different problems, and different people. For the management reporting to be of value it must take account of these differences.

Similarly, plants change over time and their manage-ment reporting must also change with them. Continuous improvement, a cornerstone of world class employee in-volvement, creates rapid and widespread change through-out an organization. Far greater flexibility and understanding is required. The traditional management accounting reports used by senior managers to judge success may show that a plant is performing poorly when, in fact, the plant is doing marvelously well. It is the reports that are wrong; they are measuring the wrong things, and this lack of flexibility can become a serious problem when the local managers are working hard to bring their plants up to world class status.

- *Cost accounting reports frequently are received too late to be of value.*

A world class company needs information on-time. The timeliness of information will vary according to the need, but it must be up-to-date and accurate. Traditional management accounting systems are usually driven by the financial accounting calendar and the reports come out monthly. The reports often come out several days, or even weeks, after the month has closed. If a report comes out two weeks after the end of the period some of the information will be more than six weeks out of date.

The average age of the information is three weeks. This is not timely and is not useful. In reality no one in the company really uses these reports to control the business; they are just too late to be useful.

- *Cost accounting reports are frequently viewed with disdain by operations managers because they do not find the reports helpful with their job, and instead, often find themselves censured when variances are unfavorable.*

Operations supervisors and managers receive a double jeopardy from the month-end accounting reports. Not only is the information late, misleading, and unhelpful, but they are then expected to explain variances and justify themselves. In many companies the variance reports are accompanied by long analysis meetings entirely devoted to finger-pointing. Operations people associate the cost and management accounting reports (and often the people as well) with another instance in which they have to fight their corner instead of working in the plant and doing something useful. It has been known that operations people may manipulate the figures to "keep the accountants off our backs."

What has this got to do with a world class company? Where is the value-added in all of this? The answer is, of course, that the entire process is waste and should be eliminated.

4. Incompatibility with World Class Approaches

- *Traditional methods of assessing the pay-back on capital projects can impede the introduction of world class methods.*

Western companies use return-on-investment (ROI), discounted cash flow (DCF), and other analysis tools to determine the viability and desirability of a capital project. These approaches are based on forecasts and estimates that are often little more than guesses. The analysis always results in a recommendation to spend a large amount of money on a large, specialized, high-tech piece of equipment that will bring a big payback over a five-year period. The engineers in the company will usually endorse this approach because they always want to work with the best and most advanced machines and equipment.

While capital investment and the use of advanced equipment is an important aspect of the modern business world, a world class manufacturer will assess capital equipment projects quite differently from the traditional approach. ROI and DCF do not take account of such issues as quality, customer service, flexibility, or short lead times. The goal of cross-training the people in the company can be hampered by introducing new machines that require specialist technologies to run and maintain it.

Cellular manufacturing needs smaller, often low-tech equipment that fits well into a small cell instead of a large, central piece of equipment that cannot be included in a cell approach. A world class manufacturer is looking to be able to make very small quantities of highly customized products—the opposite of mass production. As new products are introduced and production volumes need to increase, a world class manufacturer will often want to gradually increase production capability "just-in-time" for when it is needed. This runs counter to the typical results of ROI calculation that recommend purchase of large and expensive high volume equipment.

- *Cost accounting often causes managers to do wasteful and unnecessary tasks in order to make the figures look good.*

There are countless non-value-added and wasteful things done in a company to "feed" the accounting system. Most of us have war stories of down-right stupid things we have done over the years to keep the accountants happy. The most common scenario is the month-end production push. Most companies ship a large amount of their products in the last few days coming up to month-end. Some companies in fact back-date shipments in the first few days of a new period to the previous period because they have numbers they need to achieve.

This approach disrupts the smooth flow of the operation, often compromises quality in order to get the products out the door (to move the metal), has nothing to do with a just-in-time approach, does not contribute to real customer service, and demonstrates a production facility that is out of control. If you ask the managers why they are doing this they will reply that they have month-end shipment targets to meet. This kind of thing has no place in a world class company. Why should production output be driven by an accounting month-end? This is nonsense.

Other examples of wasteful activities driven by the accounting systems are the manipuation of stock figures to achieve month-end inventory targets, falsifying time cards to match labor hours to standards, "cherry picking" production to enhance earned hours reporting —and the list goes on. The accounting systems are making otherwise rational managers do stupid and time-wasting things for no valid reason.

- *Concentrating on machine and labor efficiency and utilization rates encourages the production of large batch quantities.*

Traditional management accounting systems carefully measure labor efficiencies and machine utilization. This is very harmful to world class manufacturing because it encourages people to make more than they need. A world class company would plan to make only what the customer requires and ship it just-in-time for the customer's needs. They do not want to build inventory ahead of time just to keep a machine running or to keep people occupied. It is better to have low labor efficiency than to build things you don't need. Both of these approaches lead you to large batch sizes, whereas a world class manufacturer is focusing on small batches, one-piece part flow, and fast changeover.

- *Overhead absorption variances encourage large batch sizes and overproduction.*

  In a similar way a company that places great store on overhead absorption will tend to build more inventory than they need. Worse than that, the people will "cherry pick" in order to build products that garner more overhead absorption than others, creating an imbalance in production and inventory levels. In addition, overhead absorption variance is a measure so complex and intangible that very few people in the company really understand it—let alone see its relevance—so the people are being driven by something they don't understand to do things that harm the company and do not serve the customers.

- *Cost accounting requires much detailed data that is costly to obtain.*

  The cost of obtaining the information required by a traditional cost accounting system is enormous and unmeasured. Very few companies would be able to measure the cost of their costing system. In most companies the managers would not think about asking the question because the cost and management accounting systems are so ingrained into the company and its thinking that it is difficult to question it, and almost impossible to simplify and eliminate it.

  Included in the costly and irrelevant areas of cost tracking are the reporting of labor hours, tracking of job-step completion on the shop floor, reporting of materials issued to production jobs, tracking of WIP inventory, the whole work-order process, and even reporting production completions.

Beneath the surface of a complex accounting system is some bad theory. The theory is that in order to control the business you must track and check everything in detail. The more transactions processed on the computer or in the ledgers, the more the company is under control. We have discovered in recent years that the opposite is true. A world class company creates control within its organization by bringing its *processes* under control: production, administration, quality, and new product development. Excellence and proactive control does not come from checking and tracking everything; it comes from studying and perfecting every process in the company.

The theme of this entire book is to move accountants away from detailed bookkeeping, tracking, and checking; and give them the tools to help create excellence in the company's operations. As Robin Cooper pointed out, "just as you cannot inspect quality into a product, you cannot account costs out of it." (Cooper 1995)

• *Cost accounting reinforces the entrenched ideas and outmoded methods that need to be replaced.*

A common notion holds that accountants are conservative by nature, reluctant to innovate, and therefore obstruct progress. Such is not necessarily the case. When a company implements world class manufacturing, just-in-time, or agile methods the accountants are often the people who immediately appreciate the benefits of the changes and participate fully in the implementation.

It is true that in many companies that have been successful with world class manufacturing techniques, the accounting systems have not changed as quickly as the production techniques and have become a hindrance to the progress of improvement. Sometimes the accountants feel it is their responsibility to act as internal watchdogs and validate the changes before they go along with them. In addition, cost and management accounting systems are frequently complex and thorough and it is not easy to modify or dismantle them, particularly in a larger, multi-site organization.

Another problem is that accountants have been trained to observe tried and tested accounting practices and there are no new standards for the role and practice of the accountant in this new environment. The accounting bodies have been slow to provide guidance or training in these new concepts. At a time when production personnel have been going through significant retraining in the ideas of lean manufacturing, total quality management, and other world class methods, there has been little opportunity for the accountants to be retrained in their disciplines.

5. Inappropriate Links to the Financial Accounts

- *Too often the cost accounts are regarded as a subsidiary ledger of the financial accounts. To be of value, management accounting systems must be based on different methods and assumptions than the financial accounts. These methods apply to such issues as inventory valuation, overhead absorption, and accounting periods.*

A traditional company had long production cycle times and large inventories and, therefore, required detailed systems to support the valuation of inventory, raw materials, work-in-process, and finished goods. A world class company strives to make cycle times very short and inventories very low. These initiatives are not taken primarily to save money; they are taken to serve the customers quickly, effectively, and flexibly. As a company moves into low inventory, short cycle time production there is no need to keep detailed track of materials and certainly no need to track the inventory value in detail.

The traditional idea of posting inventory value across to the balance sheet at standard or actual cost is no longer significant. Inventory values can be posted in macro terms based on receipt costs minus stock issues and scrap. Or the inventory can be valued once and kept the same until something significant changes in the company's business. There are several ways of handling these issues that do not require integrating the financial accounts and the management accounts.

Similarly, the full absorption of overhead costs into inventory does not need to be done individually for each product and quantity held in stock. This can be done in macro terms for financial accounting purposes and does not require linking the cost and management accounting system to the financial accounts.

Typical monthly accounting reports are not useful in a world class manufacturing environment. If a monthly cycle is required for the financial accounts there is no reason why this should be true for the management accounts. Worse than this, in many companies the confusion is exacerbated by the use of the fiscal calendar quarterly (4:4:5 week) accounting cycle, and some companies have different calendars for production, forecasting, sales and marketing, and accounting. World class manufacturing looks for simplicity; tying management accounts to the financial accounting cycles has no value.

An incisive criticism of Western managers is their short-term thinking. Financial accounting supports and feeds this short-term approach. In many cases these approaches are forced on the company by stockholders, market analysts, company board members, and the like. There is no reason why the management accounting systems should be included in this short-term-ism. World class manufacturers are looking for gradual improvement day-in and day-out through continuous improvement, and for radical improvements through reengineering entire processes. It took the major Japanese companies 30 or 40 years to achieve the world class manufacturing methods that created a revolution in the West in the 1980s. It often takes a long time before the improvements made through world class manufacturing methods hit the balance sheet and the P&L; there may be short-term negatives. World class operations require a long-term strategy.

Summary

Traditional management accounting was developed during the industrial revolution and the early part of the twentieth century. The techniques of management accounting have not significantly changed since the 1930s, when industry-wide standards were adopted. Enormous changes have taken place in technology and production techniques, and the old style of management accounting is no longer useful. At best it is irrelevant, and often it is positively harmful.
The primary problems with traditional accounting include:

- Lack of relevance to manufacturing strategy, the daily control of the business, and product pricing decisions.
- Cost distortion caused by inaccurate understanding of cost patterns, by not distinguishing direct and indirect costs properly, and by apportioning overheads incorrectly.
- Inflexibility because the methods and reports do not vary from plant to plant and from time to time, and because the reports are too late to be of value.
- Incompatibility with world class approaches by assessing capital projects incorrectly, concentrating on machine and labor efficiencies, encouraging large batch sizes, causing managers to do wasteful activities, and maintaining wasteful and obsolete systems.
- Inappropriate links to the financial accounting system, which causes confusion and makes cost and management accounting information less useful.

Questions

1. Why do accounting methods need to change from the time-honored techniques of traditional accounting?

2. What changes need to be made in the way financial accounting is done by the company?

3. Why is traditional management accounting irrelevant to a company that is moving into world class manufacturing methods?

4. What causes product cost distortion when using a traditional standard cost system?

5. Why does traditional accounting impede progress towards world class manufacturing?

6. Why do most companies tie the management accounts into the financial accounts?

3

World Class and
Agile Manufacturing†

World class manufacturing is a loosely defined term that captures the all-embracing changes that have been taking place in Western manufacturing industry over the last fifteen to twenty years. Prompted by competition from radically better companies, particularly Japanese companies, Western manufacturers have had to take a close look at their business approach and practices. This has not been easy for many companies. The three decades after World War II were halcyon times for American industry. With rich resources, a well-educated work force, superior technology, a large home market, and an excellent industrial infrastructure, American manufacturers dominated the world.

These successes were based on the concepts of mass production pioneered so brilliantly in the 1920s by Henry Ford and General Motors. But during the 1970s vibrant Japanese companies began to

---

† This chapter presents the concepts of world class manufacturing and agile manufacturing. Readers who are anxious to get to the practical issues of simplifying accounting systems may want to skip this chapter and proceed directly to Chapter 4.

infiltrate the American and European markets with high quality, low price products with superior designs. Within a few short years some Western industries (cameras, for example) were destroyed and others (automotive, for example) were radically changed by the entrance of competitors from Japan and other Pacific rim competitors. What these new competitors brought with them were the ideas of lean or world class manufacturing. Lean manufacturing was built upon the idea that high quality products could be made at low cost in small quantities. This was the opposite of the American mass production approach and required a clearly different vision and philosophy.

What Is Real Manufacturing?

The basic ideas of manufacturing are quite simple. Where does wealth come from? Wealth comes from digging stuff out of the ground, heating it up, banging it around, making it into something people need or want, putting it in a box, and shipping it to the customer. Wealth is not created in banks, schools, insurance companies, shops, or service industries. Wealth is only created by making things. And the countries that are going to prosper need to be very good at creating wealth through making things. The issues of world class manufacturing are very important to Western countries because, as we move into the twenty-first century, it is those countries that have a vigorous and effective manufacturing industry that are going to be wealthy, have political power in the world, and maintain the freedom that former generations fought for. There is more at stake than just maintaining jobs and making money.

The Issues of World Class Manufacturing

There are four cardinal aspects of world class or lean manufacturing:

- Quality
- Just-in-time manufacturing

- World class people
- Flexibility

These issues are in a sequence that represents the degree to which these ideas have been implemented in Western manufacturing companies. Almost every company (more than 85 percent according to a recent survey) has gotten the message on quality. This does not mean that they have achieved high quality products and services yet, but it does mean that most Western companies have a clearly defined quality program at work within their organization that is bringing the ideas of *total quality management* into reality throughout the organization.

It is similar with just-in-time manufacturing (JIT); more than 50 percent of American companies claim to be implementing some aspects of just-in-time manufacturing (White 1993). This may represent many companies with only a crude notion of JIT, but nonetheless it shows that many companies are taking JIT seriously. Back in the 1980s when just-in-time was a new idea it was difficult to persuade managers that JIT applied to their company; these days there is no such difficulty, as more and more companies are introducing the ideas of just-in-time manufacturing in a wide variety of industries and situations. The people aspects, however, are not nearly so well advanced within American corporations because they are much more difficult to implement and require a long-term dedication to the ideas of team-work and empowerment.

The last major category is flexibility. Very few Western companies are addressing the issues of flexibility very seriously. This is not an indictment; the fact is that most companies are working hard to bring high quality, just-in-time, and other advanced methods into their companies, and the ideas of flexibility are taking a back seat. But flexibility is very important and will be an increasingly important element of competitiveness as we move into the twenty-first century. Many of the better Japanese (and other Pacific rim) companies are focusing on flexibility as one of their competitive edges over the next five years. As Western competitors begin to make improvements in quality and just-in-time manufacturing methods, these companies are seeing flexibility as one of the keys to continued excellence.

Quality

Quality is a way of life in world class manufacturing. The approach taken to quality is quite different from that of traditional manufacturers because world class manufacturing is not only concerned with detecting quality problems but also with resolving the problems at their source. A traditional manufacturer, recognizing that there will always be rejects with any manufactured item, will build acceptable reject rates into production plans and customer orders. A world class manufacturer recognizes no such "reality" and sets the quality goal at zero defects or 100 percent quality. This level of quality is achieved through a systematic, long-term program of identifying quality problems and harnessing the entire work force to resolving these problems.

A traditional manufacturer employs a large staff of inspectors whose job is to check the quality of all materials purchased from vendors and everything manufactured within the plant. Subassemblies are inspected at each stage in the production process to ensure that they "pass." The thinking behind this approach has always been to ensure quality by having the product quality inspected at each stage in the production process by independent, trained quality inspectors and thereby ensuring the quality of the final product sold to the customers.

This approach is not only expensive, it is also ineffective. Many companies have learned that improved quality does not come from having more inspectors. The production staff does not feel that quality is its responsibility if its work is inspected by others throughout the process. The inspection department is considered to be responsible for product quality. This situation becomes untenable for all concerned. Inspectors become increasingly frustrated because they are held responsible for something over which they have no control. Production people are equally frustrated because they have people looking over their shoulders all the time checking up on them and assigning blame when things go wrong.

A world class manufacturer places responsibility for quality with the people who do the job. Pride of ownership is fostered on the shop floor because people have both the authority and the responsibility for quality. Craftsmen have always taken pride in their work because they feel the products in some way represent themselves. Much of this outlook has been lost as modern industry developed from craft-based enterprises to factory-based production. World class manufacturers can engender this kind of pride and personal responsibility within the production force and beyond. For this approach to be successful, the people responsible for quality must have the tools, training, and authority available to them to create zero defects. A number of techniques that lend themselves to this approach are widely used. These techniques include statistical process control (SPC), the posting of quality results on the shop floor as they occur, quality circles where quality problems can be analyzed and resolved, and appropriate education and quality standards that emphasize the importance of quality to the company. Of paramount importance is a standard approach to the analysis and resolution of quality problems within the organization so that every team has common methods for creating total quality management (TQM) within their area of responsibility.

The quest for quality does not end on the shop floor. Every department within the company is affected by the need for zero defects. Because quality starts with a product that is designed for quality, many world class organizations stress quality through the product design process. This change requires a much closer link between the design engineers, the people who make the product, the customers, sales people, and accountants. Some companies, including some of the very best Japanese companies, have developed an approach called *concurrent engineering* where a cross-functional team (often including customer and supplier representatives) works together to design a new product. The purpose of these teams is to design the products the customers want, to produce products at a price they are willing to pay, to achieve 100 percent quality, and to bring these innovative new products to market very quickly. This ambitious objective has been highly successful in many companies. Sales people, marketing people, design engineers, production engineers, accountants, field service people, shopfloor people, and administrative staff work together in dynamic "tiger teams" to develop new products and launch them onto the market. (See Chapter 8.)

The results have been phenomenal. New products have been introduced at a fraction of the time, product quality becomes radically better, the design is "right first time" because a range of skills contributing to the design ensures all aspects are fully considered, and the company is introducing products the customers want to buy.

Just-in-Time Manufacturing

Just-in-time—a cornerstone of world class manufacturing—is another term that has become common parlance in the last few years. JIT is concerned with the elimination of waste, where waste is defined as any activity that increases cost without adding value to the product being manufactured or the service being provided. The objective of JIT manufacturing is to change the production process to eliminate waste. Emphasis is placed on eliminating inventory, not only because inventory is an expensive waste in itself, but also because high levels of inventory have traditionally been used to hide numerous problems within the company. These problems include poor quality, poor planning and scheduling, inaccurate records, poor design, unreliable suppliers, unpredictable production yields, and so on.

Another emphasis of just-in-time manufacturing is on short production cycle times. Long cycle times require high work-in-process inventory. Long cycle times mean that products are delayed in queues, in planning, in WIP inventory, in material movements, and in inspection. All these activities are wasteful in themselves; and they also require complex and expensive systems for tracking and controlling the materials on the shop floor. Short cycle times allow you to make today what the customers want today instead of making large batches and storing them in finished goods inventory. If the production area can be set up to make small quantities very quickly— meaning that the production cycle time is shorter than the lead time offered to the customer—then the company can make-to-order (with no need for finished goods inventory) and can be much more responsive to the changing needs of the customers.

These are some of the issues of just-in-time manufacturing:

1. Shopfloor Layout and Cellular Manufacturing

Traditional manufacturing plants are laid out by function, with all the machines or workstations associated with a single aspect of production clustered together. A production order is completed by moving the materials from one work center to another as various operations are performed and the batch of product gradually completed. Very often there are subassemblies or fabricated parts that are manufactured in batches and then put into a stockroom awaiting use in a later production work order. This kind of production is very wasteful. It requires a lot of movement of materials, large batch sizes, queues on the floor, high work-in-process inventories, and a lack of teamwork caused by the division into separate departments.

World class manufacturers usually adopt cellular manufacturing methods where all the machines, equipment, and people required to manufacture a product are located together. The entire product, or a major part or subassembly, is made in the cell. Cellular manufacturing eliminates the movement of materials because all the work is done within the relatively small cell. The production is completed in small batch quantities, ideally batches of one (known as *single piece part flow*), with very short production cycle time because only small quantities are made at a time. The Toshiba Notebook computer I am using to write this book was manufactured in a batch of 10. The President of Toshiba is well known for his policy of reducing batch sizes relentlessly, and is reported to comment about batch sizes every time he visits the plant.

Cellular manufacturing also reduces work-in-process inventories because the batches are small and the cycle times are short, and there is very little inventory queued in the cell. Cellular manufacturing creates teamwork because the people in the cell must work together as a team to manufacture the products. There is a great deal of interdependency among the people, and the team members are given considerably more responsibility and authority than is usual with traditional manufacturing methods. There is no need for the complex paperwork and detailed transactions that are characteristic of traditional approaches because the material is in the cell for a short time and the product process is more predictable. Product quality is also improved through this kind of shopfloor layout; partly because the people in the cell are responsible for the quality of the entire product and also because the item manufactured in one production step is used immediately by the next person in the process. This means that any quality problems are identified immediately and corrected before large quantities of reject product is made.

None of these improvements happen by magic. The establishment of cellular manufacturing and production teams takes a great deal of careful planning and detailed calculation of the "correct" layout to achieve the optimum production cycle time (or *takt time* as it is known). Cellular manufacturing can only work well when there are standard production procedures and high levels of training and team work within the cell so that the principles of *total quality management* are fully applied. Nonetheless cellular manufacturing, in one form or another, can be readily applied to almost all manufacturing processes and invariably creates substantial improvement in quality, flexibility, customer service, and cost reduction.

2. Setup Time Reduction

Small batch sizes are essential to successful cellular manufacturing, low inventories, short cycle times, and improved customer service. Traditional manufacturers usually make large batches in an attempt to gain "economies of scale." The argument is that it takes a long time to set up a machine or changeover from one product to another and, therefore, a large quantity must be manufactured each time to ensure low costs and high equipment utilization. But a world class manufacturer reverses this argument and says that setup times must be savagely reduced to allow for the manufacture of small quantities.

These fast changeovers can be achieved by applying the concepts of *single minute exchange of dies* (SMED), a method of analyzing machine setups that allows the operators to carefully examine each step in the changeover process and cut out wasteful tasks and time delays. All production plants have their problems with machines or processes that have stubborn changeovers, but generally changeover times can be readily reduced by 75 percent to 90 percent by careful, detailed analysis and minor modifications to the equipment. Cutting a changeover from, for example, four hours to fifteen minutes makes it possible to manufacture very small batch quantities effectively and at low cost.

3. Synchronized Manufacturing

The causes of high WIP inventories are large batch sizes, long cycle times, and production queues. Production queues are caused by a lack of balance throughout the plant so that the next work center is unavailable when a batch of product has been completed in the previous work center. Some queues are fostered deliberately so as to ensure that the people and the equipment in the factory always have plenty of work to keep them busy.

A world class manufacturer is concerned to keep cycle times very short and to keep WIP inventories very low. This is achieved through *synchronized manufacturing*. When production is synchronized through the plant the materials and products flow evenly through the production cells and never stop for a moment. The various cells and activities within the cells are carefully planned so that there is a similar turnaround time at each step in the process. This synchronization ensures that the material flows through the production facility according to a fixed and planned "drum beat" or *Hiejunka* rate. When one final assembly cell is fed by one or more upstream cells, the production rates of the cells are synchronized so that as the final cell finishes one product (or batch of a product) the feeder cell is precisely ready with the requirements for the next batch. This synchronization is achieved through careful planning and cell design, and by scheduling to ensure synchronization.

Tied into the ideas of synchronized manufacturing is the planned level loading of a cell. When the production requirements are calculated to meet the needs of the customers, the production rates of all the cells and the delivery rate of materials and components from suppliers are established at precisely the rate required to achieve the final assembly schedule. This way none of the cells will build inventory and none of the cells will be delayed owing to lack of materials.

Often small amounts of buffer stock are used (in the form of two or three kanban quantities) between cells to provide some insurance against the synchronization going awry. Similarly a small amount of buffer of purchased materials and components may be held; but these "safety stocks" are very small in comparison to traditional inventory management methods.

4. Inventory Pull

A philosophical difference between traditional manufacturing and cellular manufacturing is tied up with the idea of inventory *pull* vs. *push*. A traditional company, often employing a manufacturing resource planning system (MRPII), will push production through the manufacturing plant based upon the production schedules calculated by the master scheduling system and materials requirements planning (MRP) system. A just-in-time approach allows only the customer requirements to pull production through the plant according to the current needs of the customers. No production is initiated until there is a customer order, and the production quantity is set by the customer need for that day. The jargon is "make today what the customers want today; no more and no less." This approach results in little or no inventory build up, either of finished goods, work-in-process, or raw materials because the materials and products are only made when they are needed and only in the quantities currently required. This is the *just-in-time* approach; supplying and making just-in-time.

This is fundamentally different because the production floor is not driven by a plan; it is driven by real customer needs. Nothing is made to stock; neither finished goods nor interim sub-assemblies. Everything made just-in-time when it is needed. Subassemblies are *pulled* from upstream feeder cells when they are needed in final assembly. Raw material and components are pulled from suppliers each day when they are needed. While there are often a few problem parts that cannot be pulled according to this approach and have to be handled more traditionally, a world class manufacturer will have the vast majority of production pulled through the plant smoothly and systematically in response to customer needs.

The mechanism often used to facilitate the pull system, and to authorize the production and movement of products and materials, is the use of *kanban* cards. This method was pioneered by Toyota Motors in Japan and is a simple idea. Instead of having a production planning system (computer or manual, but usually computer) schedule production, the manufacture of a finished product is initiated by the final assembly cell receiving a request via a kanban card, to build a quantity to fullfill the customers' orders. The materials and components are pulled from upstream cells and the suppliers by the final assembly cell passing kanban cards to the people supplying the materials. These kanban cards authorize the upstream cell to move a quantity of materials (or subassemblies) to the final assembly cell and to make another batch of those materials if they are required. Similarly the kanban card is used to authorize the suppliers to deliver a small batch of the material required by the plant.

The kanban card has a standard (but small) batch quantity associated with it, and often the container of the items is designed to hold just the correct kanban quantity. This way small batches of materials are moved around the plant in accordance with the production needs to satisfy the customers immediate requirements. Often the kanban is not physically a card. The container used to store the items can be used as the kanban by having the information printed on the container itself (item number, quantity, supplying location, requesting location, etc.). Alternately an *electronic kanban* can be used to trigger the supply of materials. Electronic kanbans are used when the supplier is physically distant from the user of the materials and a computer system or another electronic method is used to pass on and authorize the requirement. Other simple methods like a fax or an e-mail are also used in place of a printed kanban card. Kanban facilitates synchronized manufacturing and inventory pull production.

5. Total Productive Maintenance

A world class manufacturer cannot take a just-in-time approach without having excellent tools and equipment. This does not necessarily mean having the latest and highest tech machines and equipment—indeed, many world class manufacturers deliberately use older style equipment that people can readily understand and use (and is paid for)—but it does mean having a maintenance program that keeps all the tooling and equipment in perfect condition and ready for use. This may sound unglamorous, but *total productive maintenance* (TPM) is an exciting and innovative approach to a mundane problem.

TPM puts the responsibility for machine, equipment, and tooling maintenance with the shop floor operators, not with the maintenance department. As a part of the empowerment and cross-training initiatives the operators are trained to do routine maintenance and inspection of their equipment, and gradually they are trained to do more substantial maintenance tasks. The maintenance department ceases to be responsible for maintaining the equipment; they become the trainers, the coaches, and the specialists handling the more complex and specialist repair tasks on behalf of the operations people.

This integration of the operator's activities with preventive maintenance enhances the effort to make quality the personal responsibility of each person within the plant, encourages a team-based approach, prevents the maintenance department being a separate, self-contained entity, and provides much more timely maintenance, better quality, and lower costs.

6. Industrial Housekeeping

Another seemingly mundane issue that has wide implications within the plant is the introduction of industrial housekeeping, also known as 5S. The purpose of industrial housekeeping is to promote high quality, efficiency, and safety through a clean, tidy, and efficiently ordered workplace. Everybody in the plant is trained to keep their work station uncluttered and orderly. This includes clearing out unnecessary items from the area, cleaning the area every day (usually everybody at the same time), cleaning, oiling, and inspecting all equipment every day, and arranging all tools and other apparatus in systematic way. This is just like your mother told you: Cleanliness is next to Godliness and there is a place for everything and everything should be in its place.

The purpose of this approach is not to save money on janitorial services. It is intended to make sure everyone has an orderly environment within which to work because orderliness immediately translates to effectiveness, to develop a pride in the workplace that instills a quality approach within the employees and to develop a camaraderie among the employees through joint responsibility for excellence in the company's environment.

This does not just apply to the shop floor. Many companies expand this approach to the clerical, professional, and engineering areas of the company. One company in the American Midwest has a rule that at 3:30 pm everyone sweeps their work area, takes out the trash, and polishes the windows. Everybody, including the president of the company, does this task at 3:30 pm every day. It builds teamwork at all levels of the organization.

7. Vendor Relationships

High quality on-time production requires a high quality on-time supply of raw materials and components. A traditional company tends to have adversarial relationships with its vendors. A world class company tries to build partnerships with its vendors. The purpose is to create close relationships with a few suppliers so the two companies can work together as partners for mutual benefit and not as adversaries trying to outwit each other.

These partnership relationships are built on mutual trust and a proven track record of on-time delivery, perfect quality, and an ability to resolve problems quickly and effectively. A vendor's ability to meet the exacting requirements of the customer is tested through a *vendor certification* program that establishes the criteria for partnership relationship with the customer. Most certification programs have three stages; measurement, capability audit, and relationship building. The measurement section is quantitative and consists of measuring the vendor's level of service in the areas of concern. The capability audit requires that the customer visit the vendor on several occasions and assess the supplier's systems and procedures for guaranteeing quality and delivery. The third level is achieved over time when customer and vendor personnel from many different parts of the company visit each other and establish close working relationships. It is upon these relationships that cooperative partnering can be built.

There is more to these partnerships than merely quality and delivery. The two companies begin to work together cooperatively to eliminate waste, to perfect the product design process, to create additional value-added services, and to create mutually beneficial programs. Among these changes are single sourcing where the customer guarantees the supplier single source privileges for a number of purchased items. The customer provides long-term forecasts of requirements so the vendor can make better plans. The supplier delivers small quantities on a just-in-time basis every day. The supplier delivers directly to the shop floor without an inspection or receiving process. Non-value-added activities like invoicing and receipt transactions are eliminated and the processes simplified. These partnerships secure excellent service, low long-term prices, and mutually advantageous cooperation.

World Class People

World class manufacturers invest a great deal in their people. These investments include education and training, especially cross-training, so each employee can do a variety of jobs; team-building to initiate improvement within the company; and participation in a wide range of improvement and enhancement activities. The end result is real authority and responsibility for employees as traditionally middle management decision making devolves to the shop floor operators and other "blue collar" people.

There is a lot of talk about *waste* in world class manufacturing companies, and just-in-time manufacturing methods and activity-based management focus on the elimination of waste. But there is a strong argument to suggest that the biggest waste in Western manufacturing is the skills and talent of 80 percent of the workforce. In traditional companies the majority of work people are (implicitly or explicitly) told to come to work, shut your mouth and shut your mind, and do what you are told. They are not involved in any decision making or business improvement, and they are not expected to understand or identify with the company's broader goals and objectives. They are a pair of hands. It is interesting that in some industries the production operators are called hands and supervisors are called charge hands. These old-fashioned titles betray an underlying philosophy that is both powerful and damaging.

A world class organization rejects these kinds of attitudes and recognizes that if the company is to succeed in these increasingly competitive days, then the skills and talents of all the people must be harnessed and focused towards constant business improvement. The shopfloor operators, warehouse people, clerical personnel, field sales and service people, product designers—all must work together to create excellent products that provide the customers with excellent value.

1. Education and Training

It is impossible to build a great company using ignorant people. I am not using the term "ignorant" as an insult; I am focusing on the fact that the business and industrial world is changing very fast, and to compete successfully everybody must be continually retrained. As a rule-of-thumb, a world class company will invest around 10 to 15 percent of their people's time in education and training. This retraining can take the form of the introduction of new approaches and new ideas, or new ways to do the things we are doing now better. Education deals with the *whys*—the theory—and training deals with the *hows*—practical instruction.

This emphasis on education and training is not to suggest that people need training only in new things. In reality, even some of the best companies need a great deal of reinforcement of basic business issues. It is amazing how many companies move into word class manufacturing and just-in-time methods and neglect some of the basics. Their enthusiasm for radical change leads them to neglect the "bread and butter issues" like inventory record accuracy, good engineering data, sales and operations planning, and so forth. These traditional, unglamorous skills and methods need to be taught and reinforced.

Even more basic are the fundamental educational requirements for literacy and numeracy. Despite the billions of dollars that are spent on education in the United States and other Western countries many people in the work force do not have the basic 3R's. These problems are exacerbated in companies employing people whose first language is not the business language used in the company. Many organizations have added English (or whatever language the company uses)as a second language to their training options.

It is impossible to build a focused and dedicated team when the people are unable to communicate effectively. This is particularly true of companies that traditionally employed immigrant labor because they were low cost employees, and now find that they must change the company's culture into a quality-driven, customer-focused, team-based organization. The need for basic education is paramount.

An underlying education program providing basic skills and good business practice is essential, but to move ahead into world class methods it is also important for the company to teach their people the new business methods that provide a competitive edge. These include the techniques of just-in-time manufacturing, total quality management, teamwork, business process improvement, and so forth. Most of these methods are very straightforward to learn (but often difficult to implement) and the initial problem is showing the working people in the company that the managers are serious about these ideas. Many people have built up layers of cynicism over the years as their managers have lurched from one *flavor of the month* business fad to another. It is important that the education and training be directly relevant and can be put to immediate use within the plant.

2. Cross-Training

The building of teamwork and flexibility into a production plant, distribution operation, administrative, or service organization requires people to be significantly cross-trained. The use of such methods as cellular manufacturing, total productive maintenance, and concurrent engineering requires considerable flexibility on the part of the people within the company so that they can become "generalists" instead of specialists. This does not mean, of course, that the company will not have experts in certain areas, but it does mean that company personnel must be trained to perform a wider range of tasks.

The starting point for this is to cross-train people to do all the tasks within their work cell. These may be production tasks like welding and assembly, or accounting tasks like payroll entry and accounts payable invoicing, or administrative tasks like sales order entry and shopfloor scheduling. Once this cross-training has been demonstrated within their own work areas, it can be extended outside of those areas to other parts of the company. This is where the real flexibility lies. If people can move from production cell to production cell according to the needs of the customers, then they can be truly flexible. If people can move from accounting to sales order entry according to seasonal work loads, then the company is becoming truly flexible.

As the company moves into some of the concepts of the *agile enterprise,* this kind of cross-training and flexibility will exist between partner companies, and people will work cooperatively to achieve customer needs without concern for which organization pays them, let alone which department they work in. Cross-training is a key to both world class and agile performance.

3. Transfer of Responsibilities

For the people within the company to be truly committed to the goals and objectives of the organization they must have some control and authority within the organization. If they are regarded, and regard themselves, as "just a pair of hands," then they will not take upon themselves the additional burdens required to become a part of the world class organization. The old style company, where all the problems were taken up the organizational tree and decisions were made by a person of the appropriate management level, is no longer effective in the 1990s and the twenty-first century. Corporate downsizing has forced countless companies to eliminate the layers of management within the organization. Unfortunately many companies have downsized without creating a new culture that gives authority and responsibility to operational people for the daily running of the plant, within the guidelines and policies established by senior management.

The world class organization is very *flat*; it has few layers of management. Authority and responsibility lie very much at the sharp end of the business; the people who are working face-to-face with the customers, the suppliers, and the competitors. These changes do not happen effectively by accident. The company must initiate a policy of *empowering* the people within the organization to make decisions and to make changes to the company's operations that will benefit the customer and the company.

As a prerequisite, senior management must establish clearly understood and widely disseminated company strategies, goals, and methods. The newly empowered workers must know both the direction and the limitations of their power. The empowerment process must be accompanied by significant amounts of training and education so that the people have the skills and understanding to make the right kinds of decisions at the right time. The workers must also be given resources. Empowerment and participation cannot be done on the cheap. The people need time to work on these changes and new approaches, they need training resources, they often need tools and equipment, and authority to spend money.

Like any manager, the newly empowered workers within the organization must have the mandate, the ability, and the resources to do what is expected of them. The result of this level of empowerment is impressive. Instead of the company having a handful of tightly-stretched middle managers taking care of such issues as customer satisfaction, process improvement, quality, and vendor relationships; the company now has an entire staff of empowered, committed, and motivated people dedicated to creating the company's strategic goals through diligence and individual responsibility.

This picture may be a little rosy, and it is clear that creating an empowered work force is a challenging long-term initiative requiring consistency and integrity of company managers. Like a rose, empowerment is a delicate flower that can easily wilt if it is not constantly and consistently nurtured. Few companies achieve the highly effective empowerment described above; but many companies have made enormous strides towards these goals and have gained great benefits through it.

4. Teamwork

A team-based organization is employed by the majority of world class organizations because teams are seen as the best method of harnessing the talents of the entire organization for continuous quality improvement. In a similar way, if authority and responsibility is to be effectively devolved to the people involved in the day-to-day company operations then empowering teams is often the best way to achieve this.

There are two basic categories of teams: improvement teams and self-directed work teams. An improvement team is used to study a specific issue that is causing a problem and, using a standard TQM methodology, research the problem and implement a solution. These teams are sometimes called *quality circles* or *process improvement teams*, or *employee empowerment groups*, or other similar names. The teams may be cross-functional, including people from many different parts of the company, to address a wide-ranging issue, or they may be a team made up of the people who work in a particular cell or work area of the company that is tasked with improvement of their local processes. These teams can be on the shop floor, in the office, in the warehouse, out in the field, or a combination of these locations. Their task is to create improvement using the company's standard improvement methods.

Most companies employ a standard improvement method that is a variation of the TQM Seven Steps approach and the *Deming Circle*. These methods are summarized in Table 3-1.

A self-directed work team (SDWT) is a more sophisticated approach to teamwork and requires considerably more skill, education, and training to be effective. The purpose of a SDWT is to have the people who do the day-to-day work in the team manage themselves without the need for a supervisor or manager controlling the team's activities. This does not mean that management activities and supervisory tasks are not done; they are done by team members rather than by a separate overseer.

Table 3-1. Two Well-Known Improvement Methods

	Seven TQM Steps	Deming Circle
1	Select a process to address and describe the improvement opportunity.	PLAN
2	Describe the current process.	
3	Describe all the possible causes of the problem and agree on the root causes.	
4	Develop an effective solution and action plan.	
5	Implement the solution and set improvement targets.	DO
6	Review and evaluate the effectiveness of the solution.	CHECK
7	Standardize the solution and then reflect and act on what has been learned.	ACT

The advantages of this approach are legion. The people themselves are not only doing the work, they are fully *responsible* for the work and (generally) fully committed to the company's goals because they are solely responsible for achieving those goals. These teams hire and fire team members, create their own education and training programs, initiate improvement, and so forth. At Saturn Corporation, a car company jointly owned by General Motors and the United Auto-Workers Union, the self-directed work teams have more than 30 activities they perform in addition to their primary purpose of making the products. As well as creating a more committed and motivated team, SDWTs are also very cost effective because they require fewer people to achieve the same amount of work, and they tend to be very effective at process improvement.

5. Participation

Woven into all the previous discussions about *world class people* is the assumption that the people within the company participate in the company's self-improvement programs. If people's broad skills and talents are to be employed for business improvement, then they must participate. If teamwork is to be effective the people must participate. If there is to be transfer of responsibility and cross-training, the people must participate.

This participation can be formally or informally organized. If the company sets up education and training programs, initiates teams, establishes standard improvement methods, and provides cross-training, then the people will begin to fully participate if they feel sure the senior managers of the company are serious and have integrity. It takes time for these programs to begin to become effective and there are always problems, delays, and set-backs in the process, but everyone in the company will begin to participate, even without a formal and explicit participation approach.

More formal approaches have been very successful in some companies. One formal approach is to create a suggestion program. A suggestion program in a world class company is much more than the cob-webbed suggestion boxes seen around traditional companies. The suggestion programs actively elicit improvement suggestions from individuals and teams of people within the company. They are a method of transferring good ideas and plans from the people working the jobs day in and day out to the middle managers and quality improvement coordinators.

Very often these suggestion programs are linked into the improvement team activities so that the people can, themselves, initiate the implementation of their suggestions. These suggestion programs are often monitored carefully so that the number of suggestions made and implemented is known and so that the people and teams involved get the credit. Sometimes the people making the suggestions are compensated based upon the number and success of their suggestions.

Another form of participation is membership of the improvement teams. In some companies membership is voluntary and monitored. In others, people are assigned to teams. It is essential that people actively work on the team if improvement is to be achieved; lip-service will not get the job done. In reality people are more than willing to participate above and beyond the call of duty if they feel they are really making a difference and that their voice is being heard. It is the job of the company's management to create an atmosphere where people are motivated for team process improvement. This leadership can only come from the top of the company.

Gainsharing is another method of creating participation. Gainsharing is a process whereby the primary goals and strategic objectives of the company are evaluated financially. What is the financial benefit to the company of a 2-percent improvement in customer on-time shipments, for example? A program is established where these strategic issues are measured in a straightforward way and the people in the company are paid bonuses according to the company's success at achieving these goals. The goals need to be balanced and reflect well the conflicting priorities of any business. The "pay-out" is often predicated on the company achieving a certain level of profitability, and based on the achievement of minimum levels of improvement on every one of the gainsharing goals. These kinds of provision ensure that the company only pays bonuses when the bottom line is healthy and when there is balanced improvement throughout the organization.

The benefit of gainsharing is that it directly links compensation to the strategic goals of the organization. It enables the employees to see that their labors, both direct service to the customers and improvement activities, are directly benefiting the company and themselves. While excellence and participation can be achieved without appealing to the people's direct financial involvement, gainsharing provides a method of sharing the benefits of world class processes with the people who have created those benefits.

Flexibility

Flexibility is increasingly important to world class companies. The market and the customer's requirements are driving toward greater flexibility than ever before. Increasingly the verities of mass production are being violated by the needs of the customers for the delivery of small quantities of more customized products at lower prices.

The genius of mass production was to dramatically reduce production costs and overhead costs by making very large quantities of the same product, by limiting choice (any color you want so long as it is black!), standardizing production, service, and support activities; and reducing changeovers and running "economic batch quantities." This approach is just not viable when the market wants more choice, shorter delivery lead times, and rapid introduction of innovative new products. Unfortunately many companies have been forced by their customers to wider variety and smaller quantities, but have not recognized that fundamental change is taking place in their business. They are trying to provide this new paradigm of service using the traditional mass-production methods, and this can be calamitous.

1. Product Mix and Volume

There are wide issues associated with flexibility, but flexibility at its most basic is concerned with mix and volume of the products manufactured and shipped to the customers. The ideal is to make today what the customers want today, no more and no less. An important aim of a world class manufacturer is to set up the production operation so that the needs of the customers can be met immediately without holding stocks of finished goods. This requires a cellular production capability approaching single-piece part flow so that precisely the right quantity of each product can be manufactured each day and each shift.

The ability to rapidly change production capacity is also required. Cross-training is important because this allows the people to move to cells that have a heavy load and reduce capacity on cells that are lightly loaded. Many companies find that excess machine capacity is required to support a flexible production policy; people can be cross-trained but equipment is often less flexible. This leads to a capital acquisition policy that favors the purchase of more flexible production equipment.

Some companies have developed innovative methods of providing flexible production capacity over and above the traditional overtime and extra shifts. This may include the use of temporary personnel that can be called in at a moment's notice. One company employs local farmers to provide temporary production assistance. This is a win-win because the farmers are very adept at the kind of work required, and they appreciate the additional income. The number of people required is worked out by 5:30 pm the previous night based upon customers' orders needing shipment the following day, and the company calls in as many people as they require. There is, of course, an agreement that assures each person a certain amount of work each month and rotas are used to ensure that the work is spread fairly among the people involved and that each person's skills are maintained and enhanced.

Flexibility in product mix and volume requires flexibility on the part of the work force and the availability of excess production capacity. This runs contrary to traditional production ideas where specialization and utilization are valued; but the realities of the marketplace requires a significant change of attitude in these areas.

2. Short Lead Times and Make-To-Order

The days of delivery lead times stated in weeks are gone in most industries. The customer, very often ourselves as the consumer, requires faster service. Almost every company is faced with demands from customers to be able to deliver products much more quickly than ever before. Traditionally, if the production lead time was longer than the promised delivery lead time, the company would need to hold large amounts of finished goods inventory so the customers could be served from stock. And this approach lent itself to the inflexible large batch manufacturing methods of mass production.

Finished goods inventory is no longer an option to solving this basic mismatch between the needs of the customer and the production capability of the company. The need of more customers for custom designed products, the need for just-in-time deliveries, lower costs, and rapidly introduced new products into the market all mitigate against the use of large finished goods inventories. To be successful in the new market environment companies must learn to make products to order and employ very short lead times.

The need for short lead times and make-to-order production requires the use of just-in-time methods including fast changeover, small batches, cellular manufacturing, single-piece part flow, supplier relationships and certification, a flexible work force, and so forth.

The needs of the marketplace in most industries mitigate against the use of traditional production methods and require a move towards at least some aspect of just-in-time manufacturing. The same is true in service and non-manufacturing industries where the customers are requiring more services in a more timely manner, and at a lower cost. Car rental companies have been forced by their customers to provide much better service than before. No longer does the traveler have to stand in lines to get a car; you can select one directly at the lot. When returning the car you can check in and have a receipt in your wallet before you have taken your suitcase out of the trunk. The same is true of banks, insurance companies, financial services, food services, telelphone service, mail-order merchandisers, and numerous other service-based industries; and electronic communications are rapidly making these services more and more flexible.

3. New Product Introduction

The other important aspect of flexibility is the introduction of new products. The ability to introduce innovative products quickly and effectively is a key to world class performance because customers are increasingly requiring more new products more quickly. The world class manufacturer uses techniques like concurrent engineering to ensure that new products are designed fast, designed for quality, designed for manufacturability, and designed with a focus on the customers needs.

The ability to design products fast and effectively can be an increasingly competitive edge. Pressure Switches Inc. in Connecticut, a manufacturer of aerospace and defense pressure controls, introduced a policy of 24-hour design of custom switches. When a customer requires a custom designed switch, the engineers are able to design, prototype, test, and provide samples of the new switch within 24 hours of receiving the customer inquiry. This approach has been a key ingredient of PSI's success within a highly competitive and troubled marketplace in the 1990s.

Honda Motorcycles in Japan introduced a policy of launching a major new product every month. The purpose of this policy was not only to provide innovative new products to the market, but also to perfect the new product introduction process. A process that occurs regularly every month and is a standard part of the business practice can be performed much better than an ad-hoc product launch that occurs sporadically.

The Move to Agile Manufacturing

In recent years there has been a move beyond world class or lean manufacturing methods into *agile manufacturing*. The term "agile" is once again loosely defined, and much of the work on agility has been theoretical rather than practical. However, there are many companies that have moved into at least some of the methods of agility and are reaping great benefit. As we move into the twenty-first century the ability to be agile will become a major factor for all companies—manufacturing, service, and infrastructure—that need to be competitive on the world market. There are four principle elements to an agile organization (Goldman 1995):

- Enriching the customer
- Cooperating to enhance effectiveness
- Mastering change and uncertainty
- Leveraging people and information

Enriching the Customer

World class manufacturers focus on the customers' needs and ensure that the customers' products are shipped on time, all the time. The agile company goes a step further and addresses the wider issues of customer satisfaction. The emphasis is placed on the benefit derived by the customers from using the products and services the company provides. Such issues as measuring the customer's benefit from the products, the ease with which the customer uses and deploys the products, and the ease with which the products fit into the customers' business practice are addressed by companies seeking to become agile.

An agile company focuses not on selling products to customers but on selling *business solutions* to the customers. The sale of products is not seen as a single transaction, but as the creation of a relationship so that products can be customized or designed to meet the customer's specific need and to provide the highest value. The idea is to provide products of such high value that pricing issues become secondary because the customer is receiving a unique combination of product, service, and value. Product design focuses on being able to continually add additional value to the product as time goes by. Instead of selling your customer more and more products, you sell them products that can be easily enhanced by additional features or by software additions.

The value the company provides to the customer is less within the products themselves than within the additional services and added-value information that goes with them over their life cycle. The organization sells skills, knowledge, and information as much as products. The emphasis is on reconfiguring the products and services over time as the customers' needs change and as the products and their related technologies are enhanced. These skills and knowledge also manifest themselves in an ability to respond rapidly to customers' needs for new products, adapted products, and new or enhanced methods of using the products and services. The agile company will sometimes combine in-house expertise with that of third party partners with specific skills for specialized needs.

Cooperating to Enhance Competitiveness

The essence of an agile manufacturer is a company that has learned to adjust to the changing needs of the marketplace by working cooperatively within and outside the organization to serve the customers and achieve the company's objectives. The element of cooperation expands outside the company into third party partnerships.

The organizational structure of an agile organization will lend itself to a great deal of cross-functional and concurrent activity. This requires excellent communication within the organization and excellent and continuous training of the people. There must also be ready access to huge amounts of information about products, about the markets, about the technologies, about competitors, about the company. Internal information—good and bad—about the company must be disseminated throughout the organization. There must be convenient ways for everybody in the company to tap into the latest information about customers, products, production schedules, suppliers, new product introductions, personnel issues, financial information, and so forth. The people within the company must be able to make decisions based on true business benefits; not on such issues as volumes and margins. For a company to be agile its people must be highly educated and highly informed.

Agile organizations prize partnership relationships. They recognize that no company can have all the skill, knowledge, and expertise to serve the customers in the most beneficial way, and they find partners to work with. Their first choice is to move into a partnership relationship to serve a customer or exploit a market. These relationships often form *virtual corporations* that exist for a short time to serve the needs of a particular customer or market and then dissolve when the need goes away. These virtual corporations are set up based on trust and respect, rather than on legal agreement. There has to be some legal structure but the agile company recognizes that successful business ventures are based on relationships and not on contracts. The changing needs of the marketplace can lead a virtual corporation to turn out quite differently from the way it was originally envisioned; the letter of the law is of little importance in comparison to the need for the two, three, or more companies being able to work cooperatively for mutual and customer benefit.

The teamwork that is so important internally within an agile organization extends to the virtual corporation, the factory outside our walls, or the design shop on another continent. Cross-functional teams and concurrent development groups between the various firms involved in a virtual corporation are commonplace because it is the virtual corporations' ability to quickly and effectively meet customer needs that makes it of value at all. The teams work on product development, marketing, sales, raw material procurement, product enhancement, and customer relationships. Very often customers and vendors become partners with the company to form a mutually beneficial organization, and it is not uncommon for competitors to ally themselves for a short time to exploit a specific need.

There are very serious issues to be dealt with when a virtual corporation is established. Some of these relate to intellectual property rights, others to the trustworthiness of the companies, and the track record of success in partnership ventures. There are significant personnel issues relating to the intercompany teams that are established: Who does each person work for and how are they "managed" or supervised? The reasons and objectives of the virtual organization must be clearly understood and agreed on so that each company involved knows what to expect of the other partners and what is expected of it.

Mastering Change and Uncertainty

Speed of change is another touchstone of agilty. An agile company makes decisions very fast; often the people working closely with the customers and partners have the authority to make significant decisions within the guidelines of the companies' policies and objectives. An agile company will have a flat structure; instead of a hierarchy there are teams of people working together to achieve customer benefit. The organization of the agile company can change very quickly and it is constantly reforming itself; in fact organizational restructuring is built into the company's culture and the organization is a hotbed of continuous change. Agile companies tend not to have functional departments because they are structured to meet the customer's needs and these needs are invariably cross-functional.

The people who thrive in agile companies are risk-takers and internal entrepreneurs. The company deliberately encourages individual and team-based initiative within the guidelines of customer benefit and company policies and objectives. The managers in the company function as organizational coaches and spend their time helping "self-starters" within the company achieve their best. Even people who try and fail are rewarded for their initiative. Information is spread widely within the company so that everybody can be "in the know" and power is not centered on a few people with access to information.

A primary focus of many agile companies is the cycle time from a concept being envisioned and cash coming into the company as a result of this new concept. The faster the concept-to-cash cycle time, the more agile the company has become. This level of agility requires a clear, inside knowledge of the customers needs, employees that are empowered to make significant decisions, an organization that allows employees at all levels contribute to a new initiaive, and the ability of the employees to see the benefits (financial and otherwise) that accrue to the company as a result of a new initiative.

Leveraging People and Information

An agile company encourages internal entrepreneurs; they are the people who create the concepts and turn them into cash quickly. They must be nurtured by an atmosphere that allows them to pursue their ideas safely, that allows them and their team to be rewarded financially and in other ways for their efforts, and by an organization that has excellent two-way communication throughout the various areas of the business. The people in a successful agile company concentrate on business improvement and the effect of their efforts on the company's success. They are also essentially team-players who like to achieve innovation and success through teams of people (within and outside the firm) working together.

To draw the very best from people, a company must invest in them. This investment includes a great deal of education and training, a great deal of communication and time spent discussing issues and explaining the company's approach to every aspect of the business, and the opportunity to take initiative and (sometimes) fail. Tied closely to this is the exploitation of core competencies. The company must have a clear picture of its core competencies—the skills and attributes that make the company competitively strong—so that these aspects of the business can be enhanced and perfected. This way the company is ensuring that it remains at the forefront of the market.

The use of information is an important element of agility. The fast, electronic dissemination of information throughout the organization allows the employees to be truly included in every aspect of the company's business even if they are geographically spread out. Fast and thorough information enables everyone in the company to treat the customers as their close and personal business partners because the customers are not strangers; the employees all have large amounts of direct information about each customer. Technology has enabled us to be closer to the customer even though we are far away!

Another element is the use of information as a competitive tool. The information content of products can be enhanced so that the company begins to sell comparatively fewer products and a great deal of information. This information can be in the form of product upgrades or a software component of the product, or additional added-value information from the company, or information (like self-diagnostics) built into the product itself that is then available to the customer when it is required.

Agile manufacturing is a big step beyond merely world class methods. As Randy Patterson pointed out, "it is necessary to be a lean manufacturer before thinking about the challenges of agility." The issues of world class manufacturing must be well embedded into the company's culture for the new challenges of agility to be approached. Agility provides such a level of customer closeness and business effectiveness that it will be the goal of all companies to be agile as we move into the twenty-first century.

Summary

Radical changes are taking place in the manufacturing industry as we move toward the twenty-first century. These changes will be led by the needs of the customers, and the changes taking place in technology, the global economy, and social structures. The first and most frightening manifestation of these changes was the bold onslaught on western manufacturers by excellent Japanese companies in the 1970s and 1980s.

These Japanese companies had developed and perfected what became known as *world class manufacturing*. World class manufacturing includes the use of just-in-time manufacturing methods, an emphasis on quality known as *total quality management*, new methods of organizing the company around teamwork and improvement, and a flexible approach to the needs of the customer.

In the west, the 1980s and 1990s have been characterized by companies small and large working hard to address these world class manufacturing issues, and to face this new competition vigorously. Many companies have emerged that are truly world class in their manufacturing, design, and marketing capabilities.

As we move into the twenty-first century the rate of change is getting faster. Customers are expecting more. The old mass production concepts are giving way to the need to manufacture, sell, and distribute small quantities of highly customized products, with perfect quality, and on-time delivery. These new approaches come under the common heading of *agile manufacturing*. Agile companies do not look at customers solely as people who buy their products; they create long-term partnerships with companies to provide short, medium, and long-term solutions to customers' problems. Product design takes on a new role. First, it becomes very fast and is integrated into the production process. But there is also a move to create modular and reconfigurable products that can change as the customers' needs change and as technology changes. These products are often rich in information, and are supported by a wide range of new and innovative services that create more added value for the customer.

Often an indivdual company cannot fully meet their customers' needs, so we have seen the development of *virtual corporations*. These are informal alliances between companies that have complementary competencies. They come together to address specific customer needs or particular markets. Companies change the way they are organized and structured so that they can reorganize very quickly and thereby thrive in an environment of rapid and unpredictable change. This ability to change and adapt requires placing an emphasis on employing highly competent and empowered people—those who have rapid and complete access to all information required to serve the customers and meet the company's objectives.

The techniques of world class manufacturing represent the starting point for companies that wish to become agile and meet the challenges of the twenty-first century. It will be a century where change will be rapid, radical, and unpredictable, and where the global market will give rise to increasingly powerful competitive forces.

Questions

1. Why is quality of paramount importance to a world class manufacturer?

2. Which aspects of just-in-time manufacturing apply most to your company?

3. List some aspects of people management that change as a company enters a world class approach?

4. Describe the elements of flexibility required by a world class manufacturer.

5. List the four primary issues of agility.

6. Which aspects of agility would be most difficult to implement in your company?

4

Simplification of Accounting Systems

It is a dangerous undertaking to recommend changes to a company's systems—especially the accounting systems. These systems are often near and dear to the people who developed them and use them. Further, every company is different and has different needs. There is no one way to make these kinds of changes.

Having said that, this chapter will present an approach to the elimination and simplification of the accounting systems within manufacturing organizations. As we discussed in Chapter Two, traditional management accounting systems are at best irrelevant to a world class manufacturer, and often positively harmful. In any event the accounting systems are very wasteful because they require huge amounts of non-value-added work and effort for very little return. One expert takes this argument even further by saying that "I believe accounting has no place controlling how people work in today's business environment." (Johnson 1992)

Aspects of Traditional Accounting Systems

To achieve its goals, accounting systems have numerous cost and responsibility centers replete with cost allocation methods; often requiring double or even triple apportionment from service centers to production centers, and from production centers to products. These require many transactions being entered into the systems; either manual systems or computer systems. These transactions, in addition to being wasteful in themselves, are also very prone to error.

Inaccuracy is introduced into systems primarily by manual error. If you want your record accuracy to improve you must reduce the number of transactions being entered into the system. The fewer transactions, the less opportunity for error, and the more accurate the records will be. This is one of the reasons why backflushing is an important tool. It significantly reduces the number of transactions. The traditional approach is the opposite to this. A traditional accountant will say that accuracy is obtained by having people check and recheck transactions. A world class company removes the opportunities for error.

Traditional accounting systems are expensive and complex to operate. They require a lot of recording of data, entry of data, validation and checking of data as well as analysis of reports and results. The production, distribution, and clerical support staff are forever filling out forms, typing in data, and reviewing reports.

What is worse is that the systems are never clearly understood by the people using them. If the systems are complex and convoluted, then the people using them will not understand them. They may understand their particular piece of the puzzle, but will not have a clear picture of the whole process. When people are using systems they do not fully understand they use them badly, make mistakes without realizing it, and make poor decisions out of ignorance.

Couple these problems with the dubious assignment of overhead costs and the complex, time-wasting, and spurious variance reporting, and you have a system that is an appalling burden to your organization. It provides information of highly questionable usefulness at great cost.

Why would any company put up with this? The reality is that most companies not only put up with this, they actually think it is the right thing to do. This is like taking a sharp knife and opening up an artery. The life blood of the company is being spilled onto the ground.

Stupidity and the Annual Physical

The time when inventory records are *least* accurate is immediately after an annual physical inventory stocktake because a huge number of counts have been made and an equal number of entries have been typed in. This process is fraught with error. The most shocking aspect is that the auditors will look at write-up and write-down amounts and accept the inventory valuation if the *net difference* is OK.

This is garbage! The individual stock levels can be all over the place but the auditors will accept the valuation if the net difference is small. This is a total misunderstanding of what is important. Inaccurate records are a killer irrespective of the net financial differences.

Why Are Complex Systems Needed?

Complex systems make sense for companies that are manufacturing in traditional ways. If inventory levels are high, particularly work-in-process inventory, then complex systems are required to keep track of what you have and where it is going. If cycle times are long it is important to have a system that enables you to monitor the progress of each job in the shop, and to give your customers progress reports on the likelihood of the products being completed on time.

Traditional approaches to quality, allowing for tolerances and scrap factors in production and procurement, require complex systems to monitor the losses and compensate for the variability of the process. This in turn leads to high inventories because additional quantities of raw materials, subassemblies, fabricated parts, and finished products are required.

If the production processes are complex and materials are frequently moved from one work center to another, if there are backlogs and bottlenecks throughout the production process, if there are queues on the shop floor, then complex systems are required to keep track of the jobs flowing (or stumbling or lurching) through the production plant.

A company that attempts to monitor the productive output of individual people will require a complex job tracking and labor reporting system, as will an organization where the managers try to control the company using financial reports, because the detailed financial information needs to be collected, collated, and disseminated.

Firms that manufacture products in highly regulated industries will require complex tracking systems, as will companies whose customers require detailed costing and quality inspection information. For example, defense equipment manufacturers and other government suppliers frequently require complex reporting systems to provide the government with the detailed tracking information they demand.

The New Manufacturing Organization

As presented in Chapter Three, a world class manufacturing organization eliminates the need for complex accounting systems by eliminating the issues that require detailed tracking and monitoring of the production process. In contrast to a traditional manufacturer, a world class company has low inventories, short cycle times, low scrap, simplified processes, synchronized manufacturing, and no need for detailed tracking and recording.

Low inventories are the result of many different initiatives that come under the broad heading of just-in-time manufacturing. These include small batch sizes, fast setups (or changeovers), accurate records, very low scrap, reliable vendors, and a balanced production flow. Short cycle times are similarly the result of excellence in many areas including low inventories, small batches, the lack of bottlenecks, synchronized and balanced flow, making to order instead of to forecast, and very high quality.

Cellular manufacturing does much to simplify the systems and shorten the distances materials are moved. The use of production cells reduces the number of departments and cost centers as well as simplifying production planning and control methods. This simplification, coupled with shorter cycle times, removes the need for tracking and recording material movement and production steps.

Higher quality of the products and processes, improved accuracy of information, and just-in-time supplier deliveries makes inventory planning easier. Making to order rather than making to forecast is achieved because manufacturing cycle times are reduced. Any company making to forecast must hold extra inventory because the forecasts are always wrong—making to order reduces inventory.

World class manufacturers treat their people differently. The emphasis is on teamwork, cross-training, and flexibility. Instead of the traditional hierarchical management structures, authority and responsibility are given to teams who are providing products and services to the customers through manufacturing, distribution, design, and administration. The organization is flattened with everyone having personal responsibility for quality and serving the customer. People are cross-trained so they can make a more flexible contribution to the organization. Cross-functional teams are established to solve problems, design products, and to meet customers needs. Under this approach the detailed monitoring of individuals is nonsense, and the distinctions between direct and indirect labor are hazy and unhelpful, as are the ideas of fixed and variable costs.

Low inventories, short cycle times, and cross-trained work teams dedicated to customer service result in great flexibility and responsiveness to customer needs. This characterizes world class manufacturing more than any other single feature. The entire organization is built around the idea of fast and flexible customer service. Complex accounting systems play no role in this environment.

New Accounting Goals

The accounting goals of a world class manufacturing organization include paring the accounting systems down so they provide only relevant information and require a minimum amount of effort to obtain the information. This is achieved through the radical elimination of wasteful accounting processes, the alignment of cost centers to the organization's information needs, and reduction of transactions.

Another primary goal of the accounting systems in a world class manufacturing organization is to provide information that helps to improve the quality of products and services, reduce the variability of the processes, and enhance customer service. This is a different way of thinking about accounting information. A traditional company regards the accounting information, and particularly the performance measures, as ways of monitoring people to ensure they are meeting objectives and budgets. The new approach to management accounting sees the information as the servant of the people in the quest for manufacturing, distribution, and customer service excellence.

When this is done the accounting system can provide valuable information yet be much less costly and wasteful. The information is more understandable because it relates directly to the way the products are made and services provided. The elimination of complex systems and particularly the elimination of transactions immediately makes the data more accurate and pertinent.

A spin-off is that simplified systems are easier for people to understand, and when people understand the information they can make better use of it. Complex systems produce baffling reports and information that creates confusion instead of enabling people to improve the processes. Simplification creates clarity and visibility, which in turn creates understanding. This understanding fosters improvement.

The accounting information must be relevant, minimal, clear, visible, and foster improvement. These are the goals of the new approach to accounting within a world class manufacturing organization.

A Four-Stage Approach to Simplification

It is usually difficult to extricate a management accounting system from a traditional organization. But as the organization goes through the process of implementing a world class change the simplification of the accounting systems must follow the changes taking place on the shop floor, in the warehouse, and in the office. The following is a four-stage approach to the elimination of wasteful and complex management accounting methods. These changes can be made when just-in-time manufacturing, total quality management, and other world class manufacturing methods are introduced.

This suggested approach will not be right for every company. It is given as a logical approach to accounting simplification that is congruent with the thinking of world class companies. It is also intended to be a radical approach. Each organization must develop its own approach and implement the changes at a pace consistent with the company's world class goals.

Stage One

- Eliminate labor reporting
- Eliminate variance reporting
- Reduce cost centers

Eliminate Labor Reporting

In the modern manufacturing environment, labor content is very small for the majority of products. A labor content of around 7 percent of the total product cost is typical in Western manufacturing when all the direct costs and overheads are taken into account. Many manufacturing companies show a higher percentage than this because the overheads included in the *manufacturing* standard costs do not include overheads outside of the manufacturing area. When all the overheads are included, the labor costs are very low indeed. In some industries, electronics manufacture for example, the labor content can be even lower than this.

Most traditional manufacturers track labor costs in great detail. Every job step of every production job is carefully recorded and labor variances calculated. This requires that production people—usually supervisors—fill out detailed time cards showing who worked on which job, how much time they spent on setup, production, rework, break times, and so on. This information is carefully collated and entered into the cost accounting system by a data entry clerk within the accounting department.

Often this is linked into the payroll system so that people can be paid according to the number of hours they worked. In companies where people are paid for production, the number of hours and the amount of product they produced (at standard cost) is recorded and wages are set based on this information. This elaborate, detailed, and expensive system is in place to keep careful track of less than 7 percent of product costs. It is nonsense to do this and it should be eliminated immediately. It provides an illusion of control and in fact is merely a wasteful exercise in futility.

The tracking of detailed labor hours is nonsense for a traditional manufacturer. It is even more unnecessary for a company moving into world class manufacturing.

- A world class manufacturer builds teams of people working together to meet customer needs.
- Small batches and low inventories are important to a world class manufacturer.
- Short cycle times and flexibility require fast throughput of production.
- Productivity is measured in terms of total output by the team of products required by the customers.
- The distinction between direct and indirect personnel is broken down. "Direct" operators spend their time in team-based improvement projects.
- The tracking of individual production is harmful in a team-based work place. It is the team that matters; not the individual activities.
- Tracking individual labor productivity leads people to produce large batches and build inventory.
- There is no time to track the detailed labor used.

- The traditional direct labor productivity calculation of standard hours and earned hours is irrelevant and harmful.
- Tracking the direct and indirect activities of the people becomes confusing, complex, and meaningless.

It can be difficult to eliminate direct labor reporting when there are established work agreements to pay people according to productive time or output. Very often traditional union contracts set people's pay levels using a detailed tracking system. These approaches must be renegotiated and better methods developed for paying people and for providing a *gainsharing plan* in line with the company's world class manufacturing goals. Most world class manufacturers eliminate the concept of direct and indirect people. Everyone is paid a straight salary and a team-based, gainsharing plan put into place.

As detailed tracking of labor costs are eliminated it continues to be possible to track total labor costs from the payroll system into the financial accounts. These total labor costs can be used to report the cost of sales and inventory valuation information required on the balance sheet and P&L report. It is not necessary to track the jobs in detail to provide correct financial accounting information.

Eliminate Variance Reporting

Traditional systems require the entry of detailed labor and material usage information to each production job so that variances from standard can be calculated and reported. This kind of reporting is the opposite of what is useful within a world class manufacturing environment.

In a traditional approach to management accounting variance reports had two purposes:

- To correctly value work-in-process inventory
- To track poor productivity

It has been suggested that the reason computer-printed variance reports are so thick (often four or five inches) is so they can be used to inflict grievous bodily harm on production supervisors who have not reached standard. This suggestion was made by someone lacking the usual reverence reserved for variance reports.

Competition—Grand Prize

A valuable prize will be sent to the first reader who can provide a single valid purpose for an Overhead Absorption Variance Report.

Fax all entries to the author at Brian Maskell Associates, Inc.

None of these issues apply in a world class manufacturing environment. Work in process is not tracked because the cycle time is so short and inventories so low that it is not necessary. The work-in-process inventories cease to be *material* from an accounting perspective. Similarly the issues relating to productivity, scrap, and waste are tracked and solved by the shopfloor people at the time they occur. You cannot wait until the variance reports are printed to take action on quality or a process deficiency.

Variance reporting always was a fruitless, futile, time-wasting task. In a world class manufacturing environment it is pointless and misleading and should be immediately abandoned.

Reduce Cost Centers

The traditional company with its hundreds of cost departments and centers requires a complex and convoluted system to keep track of the transactions associated with each cost center. As a company moves into cellular manufacturing and begins to gather costs by production cell or group of production cells, the number of cost centers is dramatically reduced.

The issue is not that costs should be collected by cell; costs should be collected (if they are collected at all) according to the needs of the manufacturing managers. The accounting system is the servant of the production, distribution, design, customer service, and other departments. The gathering of information must be aligned with the information needs of the organization.

Nonsense and Ridiculous Nonsense

This is a quotation from a standard accounting textbook.

Whilst the principle of variance is simple, considerable complications arise in analyzing the variances and bringing out the different factors which have contributed to an overall variance. For example, the wages variance may be capable of many combinations of the following variances: rates of pay, substitution, gang, overtime, conditions, extra rate allowances, revisions, idle time, efficiencies, etc. The other main variances are materials (price, usage, mix), expenses (price, usage efficiency, capacity, volume, calendar) and yield. In addition to these there will be variances due to changes in methods and revisions to the standard during the accounting period. Since all standards are interlocking, it is not possible to make a complete overhaul of the system every time a method changes. Thus, the old standard is retained and part of the variance attributed to methods changes and revisions.

Is this nonsense or what? How does this help you serve the customer better?

Stage Two

- Eliminate detailed job step reporting
- Eliminate WIP inventory reporting
- Establish backflushing

Eliminate Detailed Job Step Reporting

Manufacturing companies with long cycle times and high work-in-process inventories require detailed reporting of each production job step because the production jobs are on the shop floor for a long time. If the jobs are in production a long time it is necessary to be able to track where each job is. The company needs to know this and the customers will often inquire about the progress of their jobs.

High inventories require detailed tracking because of the value of the inventory. A company has a responsibility to keep track of its assets. The auditors will require a clear understanding of the value of work-in-process inventory as it passes from one job step to another.

As a company moves into cellular manufacturing, cycle times are reduced, batch sizes get small, and WIP inventories fall. It is no longer necessary to track the detailed job steps individually because the products are made quickly. The value of inventory is small and does not need to be separately recorded. The manufacture of the product occurs within one (or a few) production cells instead of being trailed around a circuitous route on the shop floor from one work center to another. There is no need to keep a step-by-step tracking.

The elimination of detailed job step reporting very much simplifies the shop floor control processes because there is now very little reporting to be done. The product is reported only when it is completed, and not at interim stages in the production process. Gone are the job cards and their associated data entry.

Eliminate WIP Inventory Reporting

High work-in-process inventories require detailed reporting of material movements. In the same way that job step tracking can be eliminated as cellular manufacturing and short cycle times are introduced, so WIP inventory reporting can be eliminated when low inventories and fast throughput is established.

A traditional company must record the transfer of component and raw material inventories to the shopfloor ready for production. As the product is manufactured its progress is monitored and the actual use of materials reported. This leads, in turn, to material variance reports. When the material moves through the plant more quickly and when the value of WIP inventory is low, it is not necessary (or even possible) to keep track at this level of detail.

The first step is to eliminate WIP inventory. Instead of showing raw material, WIP, and finished products inventories, the company can report raw material and finished products only. The next step is to go to a "four wall" inventory which does not differentiate between the different kinds of inventories. There is so little material that it is shown just as "inventory."

If the detailed reporting of shopfloor issues can be eliminated, the inventory control system is greatly simplified. The hundreds and thousands of transactions that used to be required can now be eliminated together with the time, energy, and confusion these transactions required. If it is necessary to know the value of WIP inventory for any reason there are two approaches that can be taken. One approach (used by Harley Davidson Motorcycles) is to have the production process so under control that WIP inventory is always much the same. WIP can be estimated once a year, for example, and will not change substantially because the production process is balanced. Another approach is just to count it. This approach is taken by some Hewlett Packard divisions. The WIP inventory is so low that it is not a difficult task to just go out and count it when required.

Establish Backflushing

Tied in with the elimination of WIP inventory tracking is the use of backflushing. Backflushing is used when an item (or batch of items) is completed by a cell. The cell reports the completion of the product. The backflushing program does (at least) three things:

- Reports the completion and books the item into finished goods
- Updates the production schedule
- Backflushes the components and raw materials

The component backflush is achieved by reading the bill of material (recipe or product structure) for the manufactured product. The quantity required of each component is multiplied by the quantity completed of the product to determine how much material must have been used. The inventory transactions required to "move" the components from raw material into production are then created in the computer system. These transactions update the inventory levels so that the material planning systems are up-to-date and, if required, material costs can be posted to the cost accounting system. If there has been any component scrap or if there have been substitute components used, these must be reported so that the backflush is accurate.

Backflushing substantially reduces the inventory transactions reported by the system. A product containing 30 components would, under a traditional system, require at least 31 material movement transactions; one for each component and one for the completion of the finished product. When backflushing is used only one transaction is required because the component transactions are all handled automatically.

The bills of materials must, of course, be accurate for backflushing to be successful. But even when the bills are not perfect, backflushing is still more accurate than manually entering all the component transactions because there is far less opportunity for error. Only one transaction is manually entered into the system: the backflushing transaction. All the other transactions are automatic and are therefore as accurate as the bills of material. Backflushing is a powerful tool that is used by virtually all world class manufacturers.

Stage Three

- Eliminate work orders
- Eliminate month-end reporting
- Eliminate integration with financial accounts
- Eliminate budgeting

As we move into Stage Three of this simplification process we have got to the point where the ideas of world class manufacturing are really beginning to have a radical effect on the way we look at management accounting. We have dismantled most of the tried and true features of the cost accounting system and replaced them with simplified processes. We can now move on to changing the structure of our accounting processes.

Eliminate Work Orders

Most manufacturers use work orders to track production on the shop floor. A work order is created (usually by the computer system) every time a production job is required. The work order authorizes the job to be done, schedules the job in the MRP system, and is used to track the progress of production for the job. The use of a work order reflects a "job shop" style of manufacture with discrete quantities being manufactured by a specific date, often through a complex series of production steps.

The use of work orders becomes an impediment to a world class manufacturer. As batch quantities become smaller, more and more orders are required. The elimination of labor tracking and job step tracking means that work orders are no longer needed to track that information. The elimination of variance reporting means that we no longer need to keep detailed costing information for each job and a work order is not required to track the variance information.

As small batch, short cycle time, cellular manufacturing becomes the normal manufacturing method, the company becomes more like a repetitive manufacturer than a job-shop manufacturer. Although the products may vary considerably, the production processes are repetitive. A more repetitive style of production planning and control is needed. Work orders should be eliminated and replaced by rate-based scheduling or no scheduling at all.

Rate-based scheduling is similar to that used by repetitive manufacturers. Production cells are scheduled according to the rate of manufacture of products on the cell rather than scheduling a specific quantity on a specific date using a work order. The rate of production is synchronized with the rate of customer demand. Make today what the customers order today.

Scheduling can be eliminated completely when the production plant and individual cells are very responsive to customer needs. When product mix and volume can be varied quickly and easily, the final assembly cells can be loaded directly from customer orders and no separate scheduling is required. The loading of production cells that feed the final assembly is achieved using a "pull" approach. Components and subassemblies are pulled from the feeder cells to the final cell according to need. Similarly raw materials from suppliers are pulled each day according to the needs of the feeder cells. Kanban cards can be used to facilitate this pull approach to production scheduling.

The elimination of work orders simplifies the production process considerably. It eliminates the need for tracking and reporting work order numbers throughout the production process. Product completions can be reported merely by the product number and the quantity; no additional data is required. The elimination of work orders also simplifies the computer systems. The MRP can be run against customer demand and rate-based schedules instead of having to track individual production orders.

Elimination of Month-End Reporting

There is nothing magical about a month-end as far as production is concerned. Yet most companies ship the majority of their products in the last few days of the month. Why is this? It is because the production people are being driven by the financial accounting calendar. The financial accounting calendar is used to develop month-end budgets for production, costs, and sales. These are the driving force. Each manager is judged according to his or her performance against these budgeted targets.

These ideas are a million miles away from world class manufacturing. A world class production plant has a steady flow of synchronized production that matches customer needs to production capacity. There is no "month-end push." A traditional company will force a lot of products out of the door at month-end; often compromising quality, paying for extra overtime, and creating the disruption and confusion associated with expediting. A world class company does not do this.

The idea of month-end reporting of production results is harmful to companies that are driven by these results. The month-end closing of the financial accounts may have some validity to the stockholders, the Securities and Exchange Commission, or the tax man; but it has nothing at all to do with world class manufacturing.

The reporting of production information needs to be aligned with the needs of the manufacturing managers, the improvement teams, and the customer. These will vary according to the products made and market the company is serving. Different kinds of production reporting will be required at different times. Some will be needed continually, either by shift or daily, and others at another time interval. The monthly reporting cycle is irrelevant and should be ignored.

Eliminate Integration with the Financial Accounts

Management accounts are traditionally integrated with the financial accounts for the purposes of inventory valuation and establishing periodic cost of sales reporting. This is no longer relevant in a world class manufacturing company and should be abandoned. The financial accounts are, of course, still required because third parties require them each month or each quarter. However, the management accounts do not need to be tied to the financial accounts.

When inventory values are low and the production process is under control it is not necessary to link the management accounts to the financial accounts for inventory valuation purposes. When you move to a "four wall" inventory and eliminate WIP inventory reporting the valuation of inventory on the financial accounts can all be done in macro terms. It is not necessary to calculate the individual costs of each product and subassembly because the value of inventory will be the net of the sales going out and the materials coming in. The overhead allocated to the products is the total amount of overhead expenses accrued that period. It is not necessary to calculate overhead allocation variances for individual products and sum those up to the balance sheet valuation.

There is no value to integrating the management accounts and the financial accounts. Each is serving a different purpose and linking them is irrelevant and harmful. The management accounts should not be driven by the needs of the financial accounts. They should be driven by the needs of the manufacturing people and the customers.

Eliminate Budgeting

Most companies go through a ridiculous ceremony each year known as budgeting. A large corporation has a budgeting department whose sole responsibility is to be the master of ceremonies at this charade. If a company added up the cost of developing the annual budgets they would fall down with shock. It is not only the cost of the budgeting people themselves, it is also the cost of the time wasted by each manager and supervisor working on the budgets for their own departments, plus the time spent during the year fiddling the results to match the budgets instead of getting on with manufacturing product, improving quality and customer service, and creating wealth.

Every company requires a top-level macro budget. This is needed to plan the company's business direction, determine cash flow, explain the company's strategy to the investors, and provide for capital projects. What the company does not need is a detailed budget at plant, department, and cost center level.

If you read the accounting text books you would think that detailed budgets are developed so that costs can be understood and controlled. You would have the impression that a budget enables the

---

A War Story About Budgets

I was at one time an inventory manager for spare parts for Rank Xerox in Europe. I was responsible for 13 countires and 27 warehouse locations. The management accountants set inventory budgets for each country for each month, and I was expected to meet those budgets.

What would you do if, at the end of the month, you were over-stocked in Denmark and understocked in Sweden? You would move material from Denmark to Sweden. The Xerox cost accounting system was set up so that interplant transfers were deemed to have arrived when the transfer documentation was raised. So I did not have to physically move inventory. I and my first-line supervisors spent a few days each month raising fictitious transfer orders to keep the inventory levels in line with the budget.

Was this good use of our time? Did this serve the customer or improve quality? Did we even think about it? No. It was just a part of playing the game.

Do similar things happen in your company?

company to keep track of its performance and to steer each department in the way they should be going during the following year. The reality is that the budgets waste a huge amount of time, are thrown together using spurious information, drive people to do the wrong things, and are arbitrarily cut and adjusted by senior managers.

How often have departmental managers labored to create "realistic" budgets for their department's activities, only to find that an edict from above forces them to trim 15 percent or 20 percent from all their figures. Why is it that department managers do their best to adjust their month-end results to match the budget often at the expense of common sense and even (dare I say it) truthfulness? It is because a budget variance will require them to make reports, attend meetings, argue their case, and generally give them a hard time. Why is it that many budget amounts are spent in the last few weeks of the year? It is because managers know that if they do not use their budgeted amounts, they will be reduced next year.

Many approaches have been devised to improve budgeting. Zero-based budgeting is intended to eliminate the way this year's budget is a mirror of last year's. Variable budgeting takes account of the effects of unforeseen changes in the budget expenditure. And there are other refinements of the standard budgeting process. All these are merely "perfuming the pig." Detailed departmental budgeting in operational departments is nonsense and should be thrown out.

The objective of a world class manufacturer is to improve the quality of the products and services provided to the customers. This is achieved through the detailed understanding of the production or service processes and the elimination of waste within those processes. If you want to save cost, have your people become committed to process improvement, 100 percent quality, and customer satisfaction. This requires a step of faith. The step of faith is that if you take care of the right things the costs will take care of themselves. I am not saying that costs should be ignored—but they should be placed in the correct perspective in relation to quality and customer service.

This is a different way of thinking for many corporations. Management by the numbers may have been okay in the 1950s and 1960s when there was no global competition. It is not okay now. Senior executives and their managers need to realize that if you manage by the numbers you will fail. There is a new paradigm of business in the global economies of the 1990s and we must change our approach to everything. Tom Johnson has pointed out that "business performance would improve dramatically if top management eliminated all existing management accounting control systems and started people talking about customer satisfaction being everyone's job." (Johnson 1992) This is truly a revolution.

Stage Four

- Eliminate traditional cost accounting
- Backflush through accounts payable
- Electronic funds transfer and EDI

Eliminate Traditional Cost Accounting

Up to now we have considered the simplification of the cost accounting system. We will now go one step further. If nonfinancial performance measures are implemented then the production plant and warehouse can be effectively controlled without any cost accounting at all. A simple standard cost for each item may be retained, and total production costs will be tracked by adding up all the material costs and all the overhead costs for a month. We can calculate average unit cost of production by dividing the total costs by the number of units produced. This will give a broad picture of production efficiency improvement. The cost accounting systems themselves are no longer required and are, in fact, wasteful and misleading. The financial accounts give all the information required to control the business financially and the performance measurement reports control the daily running and improvement of the processes and customer service.

A periodic activity-based analysis can be performed to establish product costs and alleviate the problem of overhead distortion. This analysis can in turn be used to help with process improvement and the elimination of non-value-added activities. Inventory valuation can either be established annually because the process is under control and there is very little variation, or it can be counted as required.

There is still a need for some inventory transactions because the materials planning systems need to know the stock level of each item and match that against future planned requirements. These transactions are minimized. All transactions are waste and open to error. Fail-safe features like bar-coding standard labels or standard containers are used to eliminate error.

Backflush Through Accounts Payable

The backflushing described in Stage Two created inventory transactions for components and raw materials used for production. A world class manufacturer can go much further than this. If the components and raw materials are single-sourced then the system knows the supplier of the components. These components will be called off from blanket purchase orders from certified suppliers. This means that the completion of the product can create a backflush that goes back to the vendor. This is the logic:

- If the product was made, the components must have been used.
- If the components were used, they must have been received.
- If the components were received, they must have been called off from the supplier.
- If they were called off from the supplier, we must owe them money.

A multitude of transactions and waste can be eliminated by this approach. The material receiving process can be eliminated (as can incoming inspection from certified suppliers). The (ludicrous) three-way matching most companies do to ensure the purchase order, receipt information, and invoice are all in agreement can be eliminated. The supplier does not need to send an invoice because the backflushing can automatically create an invoice record in the accounts payable system.

This means we are getting very close to running the entire production plant on a single backflushing transaction. We still need a shipment transaction and we probably need a scrap transaction for scrapped material and products. But we have eliminated virtually all of the traditional cost accounting transactions.

If the products are made to order and are shipped out quickly after they are made, then the production completion transaction can be eliminated because the backflush can be triggered by the shipment transaction. Similarly, the invoice transaction can be eliminated if the customers have a similar automatic invoice feature as described above.

Electronic Funds Transfer

If the accounts payable invoices can be created automatically it follows logically that payment can be made automatically using electronic funds transfer. If suppliers are required to provide just-in-time deliveries and zero defects, it is only fair that they be given just-in-time payments. Electronic funds transfer is not very popular in the United States as yet, although there are some companies making extensive use of it, but it is more common within the European Community.

Electronic funds transfer, whether automatic or manually driven, saves several transactions. It is no longer necessary to print a check, sign it, and mail it. That time and complexity is saved. The supplier receiving the check does not need to enter a cash receipt transaction; the computer does that automatically. The transactions are automatic and they are accurate. Once again the manual transactions are eliminated and the quality of the information improved.

Summary

World class manufacturers do not run their companies "by the numbers." The concepts of quality and customer service are paramount. If the company serves the customer and takes care of the detailed process improvement issues then the financial numbers will take care of themselves.

There is no need for the detailed cost and management accounting procedures that are common in traditional companies. The financial accounting system provides all the information a manager needs to run the company financially and the nonfinancial performance measures ensure that the production plants, warehouses, and offices are under control and making continuous improvement.

The accounting systems should be systematically simplified as the company implements world class manufacturing techniques and ideas. Eliminate everything in the accounting systems that is not value-added—which is almost everything. Eliminate transactions; they are wasteful and create error.

Make the accounting systems simple, easy-to-use, visible and understandable, relevant, and flexible.

Questions

1. What simplification actions can your company take right now?

2. What short-term benefits would be derived from implementing this simplification approach?

3. What obstacles would you encounter when trying to implement accounting simplification?

Interlude

Accounting Is Boring but Controllership Is Not

These observations were made by Jerry Johnson, CFO of VF Corporation, at the World Class Management Accounting Conference in Arlington, Virginia in May 1991. His presentation was entitled *Accounting Is Boring but Controllership Is Not,* and it struck a chord with many of the accountants at the conference because Jerry presented some of the frustrations shared by all of us.

Somewhere back in the 15th century a fellow named Pacioli wrote the first text on double entry bookkeeping. Very few people at the time knew it. Those few who did, moreover, didn't really care. And there are still those among us today who hold the view that his pioneering effort was the first and last development of any significance to have occurred in the entire history of the subject. And I'm one of them. It seems to me that an awful lot of what has happened to accounting during the intervening five centuries—and most particularly in the past 15 years—has a lot to do with dividing up assets between creditors and owners (which was Pacioli's original purpose) and very little to do with running a business successfully.

In the past 30 years the continuing refinement of functional organizational structures linked increasingly and exclusively only by a common management accounting system has gradually stripped companies of their natural ability to adapt to change. And so, when external change presents itself for consideration, it is roundly dismissed.

My question to you management accountants is this: 'After this conference, what are you going to do differently on Monday morning?' Or are you comfortable with the notion that real world problems are going to be solved by the implementation of a new management accounting system? Or that you really believe a change in systems will lead to a change in outcomes?

Of course we're kidding here... aren't we?

One of the lessons of accounting history is that most system changes—even those thought to foreshadow monumental improvement—produced major consequences unintended by their sponsors and many created more problems than they solved.

Please don't misunderstand me. I am not against modernizing our systems. We have been pursuing activity-based costing at VF for two years and I'm very pleased with the results so far. And we are beginning to step off in the direction of nonfinancial performance measures. But let us not lose sight of the most important ingredient in the recipe for major change— YOU.

It sounds like I am beginning to say that just-in-time should begin in the controller's department—and I am. Because I honestly believe that one of the most powerful forces resisting change in most organizations is the controller. Most controllers are busy, careful about their work, diligent in supervising their subordinates, thorough in reviewing the numbers, cautious in voicing their unqualified support for any project, extremely critical in voicing their reservations, encyclopedic in their knowledge of the historical events, and generally pretty miserable people to be with.

My message is that it does not have to be that way. Despite the odds it really doesn't have to. But the difference between where you are and where you want to be is up here. *It's in your mind, it's in your* attitude. *If you and I are going to make an impact in our companies—and I firmly believe we can—then each of us is going to have to get personally involved and begin to assume some personal responsibility for change.*

The opportunity you have when you get back to your companies is to get personally involved inside the network of good ideas. Your mission is to find it, join it, and help it to grow. It's as simple as that. No script, no procedures manual, and no really solid guidelines. If you really want to play a leadership role in bringing about constructive change, you can—and you will probably have a good time doing it as well. The role of the controller is so different today than it was a few years ago and many of us have been caught unawares. Old virtues have been superseded by new requirements:

- *Knowledge must become curiosity*
- *Experience must become thoughtfulness*
- *Diligence must become dedication*
- *Thoroughness must become open-mindedness*
- *Conservatism must become enthusiasm*
- *Accuracy must become relevance*

All that remains is integrity, *which is a sufficient end in itself.*

5

Activity-Based Management and Activity-Based Costing

In recent years activity-based management (ABM) has emerged as a powerful tool for improvement. The development of ABM was preceded by the development of *activity-based costing* (ABC). In the late 1980s considerable academic work was done on the use and relevance of standard costing methods. The traditional methods of allocating overheads for standard cost calculations were called into question. It was recognized that the traditional methods significantly distort product costs and present company managers with misleading information, often causing them to make wrong decisions. This gave rise to activity-based costing, which sought to solve the problem by allocating overhead costs to products based on the activities required to create and market the product.

Activity-based costing was soon accepted as a valuable tool for more accurate calculation of product costs for pricing and decision making with a company. But as activity-based costing developed and companies gained more experience using it, changes began to take place in the approach to ABC. These changes happened for both positive and negative reasons. The negative reasons include:

- The huge amount of work required to accurately perform activity-based costing.
- The continuing debate about the relevance of ABC as an *ongoing* cost accounting method, in contrast with a project-based approach.
- The complexity of the method.
- The problem of ABC being very much an *accountant's* tool that is not relevant to others within the company.

The positive aspects of these changes came when people realized that the information collected for activity-based costing was, in fact, very valuable for understanding the company's operation and for creating improvement. Once the analysis had been done, the accountants had (for the first time) a very clear picture of:

- The processes making up the company's business.
- Where people in the company spend their time and resources.
- Where there is waste and non-value-added activities.
- Opportunities for improvement within the organization.

From this knowledge, teams of people within the company can develop better ways of administering the company's processes. They can also gain an understanding of the *real* issues that create cost, delay, and quality problems throughout the company, and seek to solve these problems.

Activity-based costing is a method for calculating more valid and relevant product costs by studying the activities associated with the manufacturing, distribution, and support of the products. Activity-based management is a problem solving, process improvement method that enables operations people, accountants, and others in the organization to analyze the activities required to perform business processes.

It is not the purpose of this book to provide a detailed description of the mechanics and methods of activity-based costing or activity-based management; there are several fine books on these subjects (see References for some suggested titles). But we will describe the concepts and purposes behind each of these approaches and show how valuable they are in the toolbox of a change agent.

In deference to the history of the subject we will look first at activity-based costing and then extend the discussion into activity-based management.

Activity-Based Costing

Most companies have no idea what it costs them to make their products. Worse than that; most companies *think they do know* —they have their standard costs to five decimal places! But they are wrong. This misunderstanding has led many organizations to make decisions that are harmful to the business, sometimes leading to complete company failure. They abandon profitable products in favor of products that are losers. No one would do this knowingly, but because companies often have cost information that is misleading and harmful, it leads managers to do the wrong thing.

This damaging information comes from full absorption standard costing, the time-honored method of calculating product costs. Full absorption costing attempts to calculate product costs by assigning a portion of the company's overhead costs to each product being manufactured. The amount of overhead cost allocated to each product is usually assigned according to the amount of direct labor hours or direct labor costs required to make the product. This was a good way of allocating overheads back in the days when direct labor was the largest element of cost required to make a product, and when overheads were small. These days—when labor is a much smaller element of product cost and overheads are very high—product costs are disastrously distorted.

The problems associated with the traditional overhead allocation methods were brought to light in the late 1980s with the publication of the influential book *Relevance Lost: The Rise and Fall of Management Accounting* by Tom Johnson and Bob Kaplan (1987). Johnson and Kaplan showed that the historical development of cost and management accounting has given rise to inappropriate methods of allocating overhead (or burden) costs. These bad methods of allocation lead to cost distortion. Cost distortion means that some products have costs which are too high and others have costs which are too low, and almost all products have costs that are *wrong*.

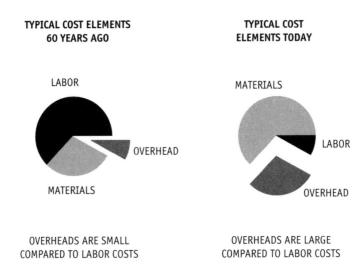

TYPICAL COST ELEMENTS
60 YEARS AGO

TYPICAL COST
ELEMENTS TODAY

LABOR

MATERIALS

OVERHEAD

LABOR

MATERIALS

OVERHEAD

OVERHEADS ARE SMALL
COMPARED TO LABOR COSTS

OVERHEADS ARE LARGE
COMPARED TO LABOR COSTS

Figure 5-1. Changes in the Composition of Product Costs

Problems of Cost Distortion

Cost distortion has many harmful side-effects. The fact that product costs are wrong leads managers to make wrong decisions about marketing, product design, capital equipment purchases, organization changes, and sourcing vs. out-sourcing. Most companies analyze their products to determine which ones are profitable and which are not. This analysis leads the company to focus its attention on the profitable products and abandon (or sideline) the unprofitable ones. The tragedy is that these decisions can be disastrously wrong when the calculated costs are wrong.

There are many examples of this. One example, described in *Relevance Lost*, involves a division of a Fortune 500 electronics company making two similar products: one for the retail market and the other sold to OEM manufacturers for incorporation into other products. Both products were similar, both had a similar labor content in their manufacture, and both attracted a similar amount of overhead. The retail product, however, sold for a much higher price than the OEM product so appeared significantly more profitable to the company. As a result, the company decided to pull out of the OEM business and concentrate on their retail product. This would have been a disaster because, in reality, the OEM product was highly profitable and the retail product was losing money. The reason was that sales and marketing costs were lumped into overheads and each of the products assumed a similar amount of sales and marketing costs. The majority of sales and marketing costs should have been allocated to the retail product. When the overhead costs were allocated according to the activities that created those costs, it became clear that the retail product was not the money-spinner they thought it was.

Product cost distortion has two principal causes: inaccuracy and inappropriateness. If there is an inaccuracy in the labor hours or labor amount assigned to the product this inaccuracy will be "amplified" by overhead rates of 200 percent, 600 percent or even greater. More important is what *drives* the overhead amount being applied. The majority of the overhead costs in a modern company bears no relationship to direct labor costs or hours. The overhead burden is made up of many different kinds of cost activities throughout the company. Few of these activities are linked in any way to the direct labor on the shop floor. To apply overhead burden using overhead rates based on labor hours or costs requires a correlation between the overhead costs and the direct labor costs. When this correlation does not exist, product costs are misleading and inaccurate.

Customer Specific Profitability

Have you ever checked to see how much profit is actually made from each of your customers? Customers are not all equal. Different customers need different levels of support. Some customers place regular orders for large quantities of products and rarely call your customer support department, other customers place infrequent, complex orders and are difficult to service. If you assess customer profitability using traditional standard costs you will not only be using misleading product cost information but will also miss the vital differences between the customer's varying service needs and costs.

A detailed analysis is required to truly understand the costs of serving different kinds of customers, and therefore to assign profitability (and possibly sales commissions and bonuses) correctly. This kind of analysis is a part of activity-based costing that provides both a better way of costing products and a clearer picture of a company's costs and profits in every area of the business.

Many people find, upon doing this analysis, that they are spending the majority of their time and effort on loss-making customers, and their best customers are being short-changed (Dixon 1992). This has led a few innovative companies to change their marketing strategy and to deliberately eliminate half (or more) of their customers so that they can serve the remaining customers better. For instance, Nypro, a New England injection molding company, gained notoriety by significantly reducing its customer base in order to concentrate on providing superior service to their few customer-partners. The graph of customer profitability in Figure 5-2 is typical of many American companies. Only 30 percent of the company's customers provide almost 100 percent of the company's profit. The remaining 70 percent of customers are either breaking even or draining profits.

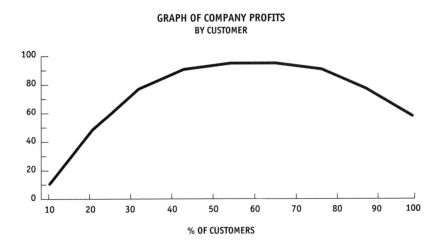

GRAPH OF COMPANY PROFITS BY CUSTOMER

Figure 5-2. Customer Profitability Graph

Making Indirect Costs Direct

The basic ideas of activity-based costing are very simple. Overhead costs and their causes are analyzed carefully so that they can, wherever possible, be transferred into direct costs. Traditional costing only considers a few costs to be "direct" costs. These include labor, materials, machine processing, and possibly outside process or subcontract costs. Activity-based costing finds ways to directly apply costs that were traditionally considered indirect overheads.

Take engineering change notices (ECNs) in a manufacturing company, for example. Would it be possible to calculate the total amount of money spent last year processing ECNs in your company? The answer is "Yes." These costs would include the engineering department itself plus numerous other costs from other departments, such as drawing office costs, the cost of placing purchase quotes, purchase requisitions, and purchase orders for the new components required by the ECN, the cost of scrapping or reworking products and components on the shop floor that have become obsolescent as a result of the ECN, the cost of training the shop people

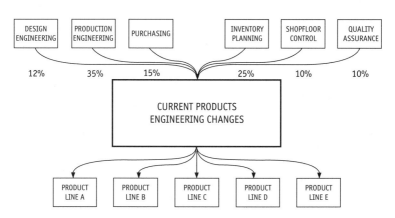

Time and resources are gathered into a Cost Pool. Costs are allocated to products based upon activities.

Figure 5-3. A Way to Directly Apply "Indirect" Costs

about the change, perhaps new tooling is required, perhaps the sales people need some training, perhaps new marketing literature is required, and new safety or MSDS information must be raised. The list goes on.

By careful analysis it would be possible to come up with a reasonably accurate assessment of the total cost to the company of processing ECNs. It would then be possible to calculate the cost of processing an *average* ECN through the company by dividing the total cost by the number of ECNs processed. Every time an ECN is processed this amount can be applied to the product (or product family) the ECN is changing. This way the ECN costs—which were formerly considered indirect overheads—can be *directly* applied to a product.

An activity-based cost analysis takes the same approach to a wide range of company costs. These are the steps:

1. The total costs are aggregated for an activity.
2. The cost of an average occurrence of the activity is calculated.
3. An assessment is made as to how many occurrences of this factor will apply to each product or product family.
4. The cost of the products is calculated based on the item's consumption of these activities.

If the analysis is done carefully it is possible to find a way to directly apply the majority of costs that are traditionally considered to be "overheads." It is not necessary when doing activity-based costing to find a perfect method of applying all the overhead costs; there will always be some costs that bear no direct relationship with specific products, such as the cost of the president's private plane. But the majority of costs can be applied in a rational way according to the activities that create those costs.

The total amount of cost does not change, of course. It is simply redistributed. It is common to find that products previously considered highly profitable prove to be loss-makers. Others that were considered marginal are in fact money-earners. Activity-based costing applies overhead costs in a more useful way than traditional costing methods.

ABC Terminology

The approach to the analysis of department costs described in the previous example is one of the classic approaches to activity-based costing. There is some standard terminology used in this approach.

Activities Activities are the different kinds of work done throughout the company. Activities consume resources.

Cost pool A cost pool is the total amount of cost associated with an activity. These costs may derive from many different departments but they all apply to a single activity.

Cost driver The item that triggers an activity. An ECN document, in our previous example, is the driver for engineering costs. Activity-based costs are assigned according to how many occurrences there are of the cost driver.

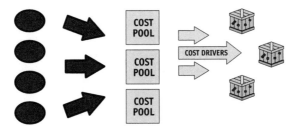

Activities consume resources. These costs are collected into Cost Pools.

Cost Drivers are used to allocate costs to products. One Cost Driver for each Cost Pool.

Figure 5-4. Activity-Based Costing Terminology

Issues Associated with Activity-Based Costing

Activity-based costing is not without its critics and controversies. A primary criticism is that it is very complex and time consuming, and that its benefits are marginal in comparison to the effort (and cost) associated with the analysis work. Tied in with this criticism is the question of when and how often to do the analysis. In the early days of ABC it was assumed that the ABC method would replace the traditional standard costing procedures throughout a company. Activity-based costs would be tracked and reported day-in and day-out as materials were received into the company, as products were made in the factory, as the various "drivers" were consumed. The amount of work and effort required to maintain this data and the analysis required to understand the implications of the numbers was excessive, and many companies abandoned the approach.

In more recent years it has been seen that the best approach is to perform activity-based costing periodically for analysis purposes and decision making, but to retain the standard cost system for bookkeeping purposes. The valuation of inventory on the Balance Sheet does not require precise costing, nor does the detailed posting of cost-of-sales to the Income Statement; these are merely accounting reports that can continue the way they have always been done. The analysis of cost variances has always been a useless and unfruitful exercise, and should not have ABC costs introduced into it.

Price estimates, on the other hand, are greatly enhanced by activity-based costs. The number of "cost drivers" consumed by the new product can be assessed, the cost per unit of the driver will have been calculated as a part of the ABC analysis, and the new estimate will therefore take account of the "true" cost of making, supplying, and supporting the product. This same approach can be extended to Target Costing and Value Engineering throughout the design process of new products.

Similarly the profitability of a product line, customer, or distribution channel will become much more valid if activity-based costs are used. The important elements that create costs in the production and distribution of the company's products and services are used to establish the profitability measures and the information is relevant instead of misleading.

How Often Should Activity-Based Costs Be Calculated?

There is no universal answer to this question. The frequency of activity-based costing analyses depends upon the company's products, the volatility of the marketplace, and the changes taking place in the company's operations. Some companies have a set schedule so that the cost drivers within the company are analyzed and new product costs calculated on a regular, periodic basis; quarterly perhaps, or annually.

Others are more pragmatic and recalculate the activity-based costs when something significant has changed in the company's operation. Examples of these changes might be a significant shift in product mix as a result of the introduction of new products, a change in the distribution processes owing to the introduction of new carriers or methods, or reengineering of a significant business process.

There are no hard and fast rules here. The issue is that the company's product costs, profitability calculations, and business cost drivers must be relevant and valid if they are to be useful. The analysis must be as frequent as required to ensure the validity of the information.

Activity-Based Management

When activity-based costing was first introduced it was seen as a method for creating more accurate product costs; and it does this. However, there is a much more important side to ABC that has now become known as Activity-Based Management. As companies began to implement activity-based costing methods their management accounting people—for the first time ever—became highly knowledgeable of the company's processes and the cost associated with them. This (in the words of one observer) gave the management accountants a *slim chance of becoming useful*!

If the accounting people understand the company's processes and know where the costs are derived, they have powerful information to help the operations people improve the operation. The techniques associated with this come under the heading of *activity-based management* and they provide a framework within which the accounting personnel and operational personnel can effectively work together to eliminate waste, eradicate non-value-added activities, and radically improve the company's processes and procedures. While activity-based costing is a useful tool in itself, it is activity-based management that can create a revolution in the company.

What Is Activity-Based Management

Activity-based management analyzes a company's processes to understand the activities that make up those processes, and the tasks included within those activities. An understanding of the company's processes, activities, and tasks provides great insight into the company's effectiveness and opportunities for process improvement. It can also lead to the elimination of waste, cost, delay, and quality problems. The primary purpose of activity-based management is to provide a standard, cross-organizational method for process improvement and measurement of those improvements. While it is common for the accountants within an organization to be the driving force behind an ABM approach, it is primarily a cross-functional process improvement tool involving many people within the organization.

Activity-based management is:

- A vehicle for creating process improvement; both incremental continuous improvement and radical restructuring of the company's organization.
- A model for showing how costs (and revenues) are created through processes and activities. If you understand the activities, then you can understand the costs. If you understand the processes, then you understand the business.
- A tool that integrates the accounting people and the operations people through the quest for improvement.
- The basis for other advanced accounting methods like target costing, activity-based budgeting, and profitability analysis.

Activity-based management enables a company to assess where they are in terms of processes that are effective in serving the needs of their customers. It enables the company to determine where they want to be in the future and provides a method for creating the changes required. In addition, ABM provides methods of measuring the company's progress in the key areas of the business that need change and improvement. And these fundamental analyses and change projects are done by cross-functional improvement teams including both operational people and accountants.

How Does ABM Help?

Look at the two cost reports in Table 5-1. The report on the left shows the customer service department's costs in the traditional way. The report on the right shows the costs within the same department by activities. Which method is more helpful if you wish to identify opportunities for process improvement and cost reduction? Clearly, it is the activity-based presentation.

While this is a simplified example, most people would agree that the activity-based report gives a presentation of the cost information that is more useful for identifying improvement opportunities. It is clear that expediting, order correction, and issuing credits are non-value-added activities that could be eliminated by improving the processes. Yet these three activities represent $520,000, almost half of the total departmental costs.

Table 5-1. Traditional vs. Activity-Based Cost Reports

Customer Service Department Traditional Cost Report		Customer Service Department Activity-Based Cost Report	
Salaries	$920,000	Take orders	$600,000
Space	$100,000	Expedite orders	$140,000
Depreciation	$100,000	Correct orders	$120,000
Supplies	$60,000	Issue credits	$160,000
Other	$20,000	Amend orders	$60,000
		Answer questions	$40,000
		Supervise	$80,000
TOTAL	$1,200,000	TOTAL	$1,200,000

Another problem is that the traditional departmental budgeting and P&L approach the organization as a series of departments instead of looking at the *processes* associated with the company. The company does not *do* departments; it *does* processes. A process is a series of activities that combine to create valuable products or services for the customers. It is the effectiveness of an organization to perform these processes—to create high value at low cost—that marks out a successful company. Most of a company's significant processes cross departmental boundaries, and it is often at these boundaries that delay and quality problems occur. To focus a company on its departments is to miss a profoundly important issue: that value is created by perfecting the company's processes.

Activity-based management focuses exclusively on the company's processes. While analysis may be done within departments, it is an understanding of the company's processes and the activities contained within these processes that is at the heart of activity-based management. If the processes are understood then non-value-added activities can be eliminated from those processes, value-added activities can be examined to see if individual tasks can be eliminated or improved, and time delays and quality issues can be addressed at the point in the process they occur.

Activity-based management is the management of improvement through the analysis of business processes, and their associated activities and tasks. This analysis is done systematically and cross-functionally so that improvement projects can be readily implemented and the changes monitored.

Putting Activity-Based Management into Practice

Although activity-based management can be used to address a specific project or process that needs improvement, ABM is more effective if it is adopted by the company as a standard approach to business improvement. This way the entire organization can be involved in ABM process improvement and (over time) every process within the company is addressed, studied, and changes initiated. In addition to creating improvement—often radical improvement—this companywide approach also lends itself to the application of other techniques like activity-based costing, customer (or distribution outlet) profitability, target costing, and activity-based budgeting.

Initiating ABM requires a successful *pilot project*. It is through the pilot project that the techniques of ABM are learned and their application evaluated. In addition to "proving" ABM in your company, the pilot project will also create a team of people from across the company who are trained and experienced in the methods and procedures of ABM. These people can then be used to initiate the implementation of an ABM approach throughout the entire company. There are nine steps required to establish a pilot ABM project. We will look in detail at each of these steps.

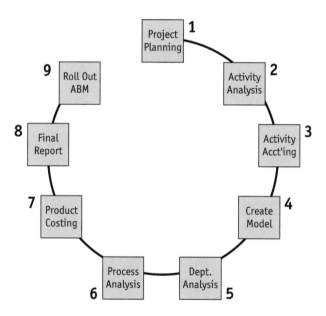

Figure 5-5. The Nine Steps for an Activity-Based Management Pilot Project

Step One: Project Planning

Activity-based management, even the initial pilot project, is a major project and requires a detailed project plan, selection of a cross-functional team, education and training of the team, and overview presentations to the managers and others within the departments effected by the project. The selection of the process for the pilot is important. It must be a significant company process that is likely to yield large improvement results; but it must be small enough and self-contained enough to allow the project team to complete the whole job in no more than three months.

Step Two: Activity Analysis

To gain an understanding of the activities performed by the departments and how much time is spent on each activity, people within the departments included within the pilot process are interviewed.

Step Three: Activity Accounting

This entails taking the activity analysis information gained from the department interviews and applying financial information to it. This will yield the cost of each activity within the department, the amount of value-added and non-value-added activities and tasks within the process, and other cost related information.

Step Four: Create the Model

Load the data into an activity-based management software system so that further analysis can be performed, and so that later "what-if" analysis can be done quickly during the design of improved activities and processes. This model can also be set up using regular spreadsheets like Lotus 123 or Microsoft Excel.

Step Five: Department Analysis

This step entails going back to each of the departments with the results of the analysis. From this analysis, working with people in the departments as well as the project team, develop improvement with the departmental procedures to cut costs, eliminate non-value-added activities, enhance the value-added activities, and eliminate delays and quality problems associated with the activities.

Step Six: Process Analysis

While great benefit can be gained by improving the procedures within departments and between departments, this kind of action is merely improving the existing approaches. Really significant benefits often require fundamentally changing the way the company operates and radically reengineering the company's business processes to bring them into line with company strategy. To achieve this, department boundaries must be ignored and the business processes addressed independently.

Using the methods of process mapping, brainstorming, process modeling, and team-based improvement, the project team creatively and radically assesses the pilot process and develops a process that is far superior to the current process. This will result in lower costs, higher quality, and faster service. These proposed improvements may necessitate significantly reorganizing the company's operation, and the implementation of these changes usually requires a wider consensus.

Step Seven: Product Costing (Optional)

Many companies use activity-based management for process improvement and do not attempt any additional product costing as such. If, however, product costing is an important requirement then it can be included in the ABM pilot project. All the data required to perform activity-based costing will have been collected by this stage in the pilot project and activity-based costs can be calculated.

Step Eight: Final Report

Once the analysis has been completed and the team has developed improved processes, activities, and tasks, then a final report needs to be written. This report will show how the pilot was conducted, present the activity-based analysis, report any improvements (usually department improvements) that have been implemented already, and present the more radical restructuring proposal developed by the project team. Also included in the report will be a roll-out plan showing how the ABM approach can be implemented throughout the organization.

This report will be presented to senior management so that the changes devised can be approved and implemented, and the roll-out plan can be put into action.

Step Nine: Roll Out Activity-Based Management

While the company can achieve considerable benefits from implementing the changes developed by the pilot project team, the real benefits of activity-based management come when the whole company uses ABM as a method of continuous on-going improvement. ABM analysis also yields penetrating performance measurement indicators that can be used to assess the company's overall rate of process improvement. An example of these measures is the value-added/non-value-added ratio. These measures are only fully valid when the entire company is using ABM.

Extending Activity-Based Management

Once the initial process improvement has been achieved using activity-based management, many companies proceed to extend the use of ABM beyond process improvement and costing. Recently developed methods of organizing and controlling the business using activity-based approaches have the potential to revolutionize our approach to business management.

Examples of such methods are:

- Using activity-based analysis as a standard part of the company decision support methodology.
- Reorganizing the company so that managers are responsible for *processes* rather than departments.
- Using activity-based target costs throughout the product design and development process.
- Establishing budgets based upon the activities performed in a department or a process.
- Activity-based customer profitability analysis.
- Extending the ABM analysis to the customers, suppliers, and other third parties so the process improvement benefits extend outside the company.

- Developing performance measurements and gainsharing criteria based upon activities and activity improvement goals.

Summary

Activity-based costing uses activity analysis to create an understanding of what it is within the company that drives costs. These costs and their drivers can then be used to calculate product costs that are more accurate and reliable for decision making. Other valuable cost analyses, such as the profitability of specific customers, can be directly derived from the activity analysis.

Activity-based management (ABM) is a powerful method for creating team-based improvement throughout any organization. ABM is a standard methodology for studying the real issues that affect the company's ability to fulfill its strategic objectives and serve the customers. Activity-based management is a tool that enables the accounting people within the organization to work closely with the operations people for improvement and reengineering of the company. The operations people bring their practical day-to-day knowledge of the business, and the accounting people bring their analytical skills to bear on the challenge of process improvement.

The ABM approach takes a great deal of time and effort, and it is essential that the approach be systematic. ABM should be introduced through a pilot project that will prove out the approach within the company, and provide a trained and experienced team to roll out ABM throughout the organization. The use of value-added analysis, primary/secondary analysis, process mapping, and team-based process improvement methodologies makes ABM a powerful tool for both continuous improvement and radical change.

ABM is an excellent foundation for a number of important and powerful analysis and improvement methods including activity-based costing, target costing, activity-based budgeting, and benchmarking.

Questions

1. Which is more important, activity-based costing (ABC) or activity-based management (ABM)?

2. What is an activity?

3. What is a cost driver?

4. Is customer or channel profitability an issue in your company?

5. Which processes in your company would be good starting points for an ABM pilot?

6. Who in your company would you select for the ABM pilot team?

6

Value-Added Management

It is important to understand the distinction between value-added and non-value-added activities. Everything an organization does is a process. The organization may be divided into functional departments for the purposes of management, but the company's processes will often cross those departmental barriers. The purpose of value-added management is to gain an understanding of the processes required to run the business, and then to deteremine if those processes are being administered well.

Two techniques are required: process mapping and value-added analysis. Process mapping is a graphical method of describing the processes within the company. Value-added analysis weighs the activities within a process to determine if that activity is contributing value or merely creating cost.

Everything that happens within a company is a process or a series of processes. An organization's success is determined by how well those processes are performed. Most companies think of their activities in terms of the departments doing the jobs, and fail to understand the underlying cross-functional processes involved.

World class companies work hard at eliminating departmental divisions. Often the companies are reorganized (or reengineered) around the processes rather than the departments. The focus changes from the departments to the customers (both internal and external). Teams are created whose job it is to serve the customers through reengineered processes designed to thoroughly meet the customer's needs.

The purpose of process mapping and value-added analysis is to understand these processes, determine their strategic importance, and measure how effectively the processes are achieving their objectives. Sometimes value-added analysis leads to radical restructuring of the company to focus the processes on the customer and eliminate activities and tasks that create cost but do nothing to achieve the company's goals. Other times it is used to create small but continuous improvement in the company's operations that gradually, step-by-step, eliminate waste and improve performance.

The accountant has a vital role to play in this process of radical change and continuous improvement by working as part of the team to map the processes, analyze the activities, provide cost information about the processes, create improvement, and eliminate cost.

What Is a Process?

According to the *American Heritage Dictionary*, a process is *a system of operations in the production of something or a series of actions, changes, or functions that bring about an end or result.* A process is a series of actions that transform some inputs into an output. The input may be raw materials and the output a finished product, the input may be a product idea and the output a design, the input may be a sales order and the output an invoice to the customer.

A process is generally initiated by a customer need, and the inputs come from internal or external suppliers (see Figure 6-1). Various *mechanisms* are applied to the inputs to create the output, under the jurisdiction of the process controller (or controllers) responsible for the process. These mechanisms include the famous *8 M's*: machines, materials, manpower, methods, measurement, maintenance, management, and money.

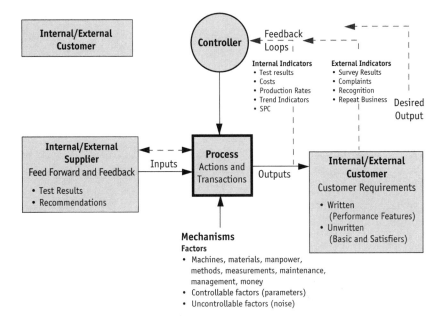

Figure 6-1. Elements of a Process

To fully understand a process it is necessary to know the inputs, the outputs, the controllers, the mechanisms required, and any feedback loops within the process. Simple processes are usually well understood but the more complex processes, spanning several departments or areas within the company, require detailed analysis.

Value-Added Analysis

Value-added analysis assumes that a process consists of two different elements: value-added activities and non-value-added activities. The value-added activities are those that directly contribute to serving the customer and the non-value-added are those that create cost without adding to value of the product or service.

A simple example of this is shown in Figure 6-2. A production process consists of a number of tasks including planning the job, moving material, waiting for the machine or work center to be available, setting up the machine, the production process itself, moving the finished item, and inspection. Of all these activities only the production process time is value-added time. All the other activities are wasteful and do not add any value.

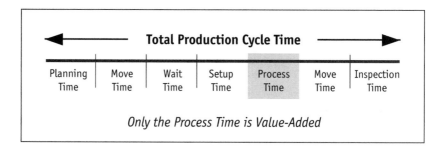

Figure 6-2. Value-Added Analysis of a Production Process

Studies have shown that within an "average" Western production plant less than 5 percent of time is spent on value-added activities. More than 95 percent of the company's time and effort is spent on activities that create cost without creating any value for the customers. A company that spends a considerable amount of time trying to improve the value-added aspects of their business by concentrating on shopfloor productivity improvements rather than by concentrating on the elimination of non-value-added activity, will actually reduce their value-added percentage. The overall effect of this is marginal improvement. A world class company concentrates on *eliminating non-value-added activities* and creates radical improvement.

Definitions of Value-Added Activities

Simply dividing the activities into value-added and non-value-added can be quite discouraging to a company or a group of people. It is depressing for an accounting department, for example, to be told that everything they do is *non-value-added.*

The purpose of value-added analysis is to provide a rational way of understanding the company's processes so that they can be improved and the waste eliminated. This cannot be achieved if the

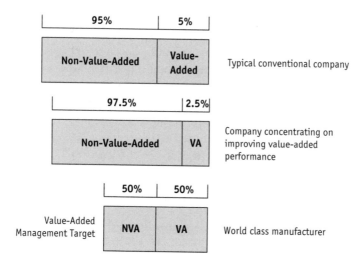

Figure 6-3. Value-Added Analysis in Manufacturing

analysis causes people to become discouraged and fearful for their long-term employment prospects.

A better approach is to provide four categories of activities:

- Value-Added Activity
- Support Activity
- Strategic Activity
- Waste

A *Value-Added Activity* is an activity that "transforms or shapes a product or service towards that which satisfies the customer's real or perceived wants and needs."

Other definitions of a value-added activity are activities that add value to the product from the customer's point-of-view, or activities that the customers would be prepared to pay for. Examples of value-added activities are making the product, performing the service to the customer, and sales activities.

A *Strategic Activity* is one which indirectly transforms or shapes a product or service and is strategically important to the long-term well-being of the business. Examples of strategic activities are new product design, training people, and marketing.

A *Support Activity* is one that does not add value as perceived by the customer but provides a service which maintains the operations process or is driven by actions outside the control of the organization. In other words, there are non-value-added activities that are essential to support the value-added activities.

Waste is defined as an activity within the control of the organization that consumes time, resources, or space but does not contribute to the transformation or shaping of the product or service. A wide range of activities fall into the category of "waste." These include inspection, scrap, expediting, and countless other common activities within manufacturing, distribution, and service organizations.

Value-Added Activity

- An activity that transforms or shapes a product or service towards that which satisfies the customer's real and perceived wants and needs.

Strategic Activity

- An activity that indirectly transforms or shapes a product or services and is strategically important to the long-term growth of the business.

Support Activity

- An activity that does not add value as perceived by the customers but provides a service which maintains the operation's natural process or is driven by actions outside of the organization's control.

Controllable Waste

- An activity that is within the control of the organization and consumes time, resources, or space but does not contribute to the transformation or shaping of the product or service.

Table 6-1. Examples of Value-Added and Non-Value-Added Activities

Value-Added		Non-Value-Added	
Strategic	**Value-Added**	**Support**	**Waste**
• Capital investment	• Material	• Quality assurance	• Inspection
• New product development	• Labor	• Purchasing	• Material handling
• Training	• Process costs	• Logistics	• Rework & scrap
• Process improvement	• Field sales		• Supervision
• Marketing	• Advertising		• Expediting
			• Inefficiencies

Uses of Value-Added Analysis

Value-added analysis is used extensively in activity-based management (see Chapter 5) to classify activities that are defined through the ABM analysis. Initially the activities are broken down into their VA/NVA classification so that potential cost reduction opportunities can be identified. Later in the analysis these activities may be broken down further into subactivities or tasks, and each of these will then be classified separately. This way it is possible to see the non-value-added elements of an activity that is primarily value-added.

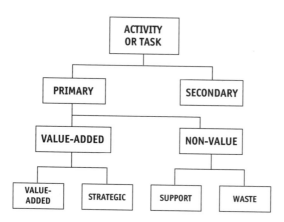

Figure 6-4. Value-Added Analysis Tree

An understanding of which activities and tasks are value-added and which are not enables the improvement team to focus on areas of improvement opportunity. Non-value-added activities are to be eliminated; value-added activities are to be improved. Improving a value-added activity includes eliminating the non-value-added elements of the activity which may be specific tasks or wasteful elements of an otherwise value-added activity. These wasteful elements include such things as delays, moving materials, setup or changeover tasks, manufacturing excess inventory, and so on.

A typical value-added analysis is shown in Table 6-2 below.

Table 6-2. Value-Added Analysis for a Production Area

ACTIVITY	$	Value-Added		Non-Value-Added		%
		Value-Added	Strategic	Support	Waste	
Direct Labor	982,440	982,440				54.4%
Dry Press Fixed Costs	67,491	67,491				3.7%
Dry Press Variable Costs	183,112	183,112				10.1%
Supervision/Administrative	62,858				62,858	3.5%
Rework	43,132				43,132	2.4%
Scheduling	58,257			58,257		3.22%
Engineering and Process Improvement	12,699		12,699			0.7%
Emergency maintenance	94,959				94,959	
Preventive maintenance	121,912			121,912		6.75%
Facilities maintenance	38,625			38,625		2.1%
Ordering direct materials	9,579			9,579		0.5%
Setups and changeovers	36,211				36,211	2.0%
Cleaning blending machines	24,141				24,141	1.3%
Inspection and QA Tests	27,463				27,463	1.5%
Rejects	41,668				41,668	2.3%
TOTAL	1,804,547	1,233,043	12,699	228,373	330,432	
PERCENTAGE	100%	68%	1%	13%	18%	

Magnetic Attractions: Blending Department

Department: 5110

Process Mapping

There are four primary purposes of process mapping:

- Knowledge integration
- Communication
- Analysis
- Improvement

A business process crosses departmental barriers within a company and each segment of the process is the responsibility of different people within the organization. To create an accurate map of this process requires input from each of the people involved. This integration of knowledge across the company makes process mapping a powerful method for truly understanding the company's activities. Frequently the people involved in process mapping are astonished at the complexity of the final process by the time they have put their heads together and completed the mapping exercise.

Any team of people working together to create improvement within their organization needs to have a common understanding of the current business process or processes they are dealing with. Process mapping provides an excellent method of communicating the current processes within the team, and at a later stage effectively communicates the changes required to people outside the team who are affected by the changes. A well-drawn and thought-out process map provides a much better method of communication than a written procedure.

Process mapping provides a standard method of laying out a process in a logical manner. This lends itself to the analysis of the process. This analysis includes not only accounting issues like the cumulation of costs and value-added analysis, but also the analysis of such issues as cycle time and quality. Process mapping provides a graphical representation of the process; qualitative and quantitive analysis information can be shown on the maps.

The use of maps for the development of process improvements has become a cornerstone of activity-based management and total quality management methods. A team-based approach to process improvement requires a method that provides a common understanding of the processes and a method to visually brainstorm the improvement of the process. Process maps provide that visual method.

Basic Method of Process Mapping

There are many methods for process mapping and it is not important which particular format is used, providing there is a clear understanding of the meaning of the symbols and the standards being employed. In some cases it is important to choose a particular style of process map that lends itself to the kind of process improvement task the team is working on; but generally the style is not significant.

All process mapping techniques use a standard set of symbols to represent the flow of work through a business process. These processes may be physical production processes, administrative processes involving the movement of documents, or logical processes within computers and people's brains. A simple and common set of symbols is given in Figure 6-5 and examples of process maps using these symbols are shown in Figures 6-6 and 6-7.

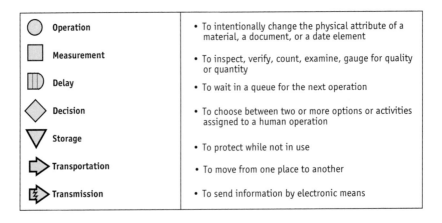

Figure 6-5. Process Mapping Symbols

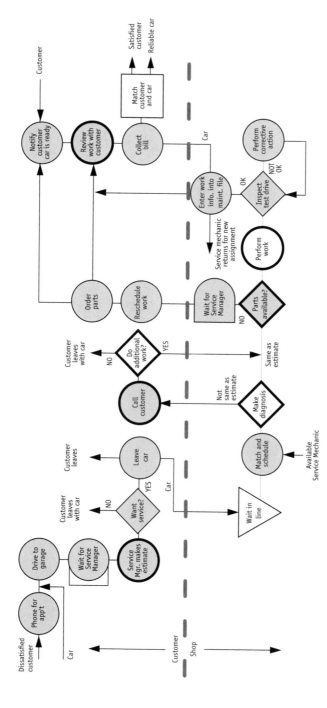

Figure 6-6. Process Map for Servicing a Car

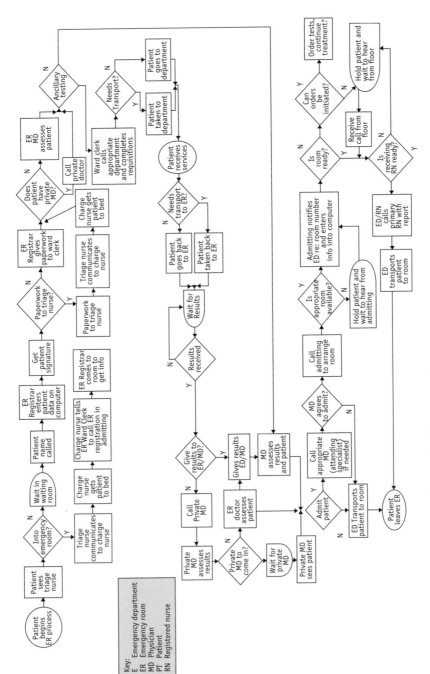

Figure 6-7. Process Map of a Hospital Emergency Room

Key:
ED Emergency department
ER Emergency room
MD Physician
PT Patient
RN Registered nurse

Basic Steps to Process Mapping

The first step in process mapping is to define the scope of the project. At first sight, this may seem obvious and easy. In practice it is often quite difficult to determine the starting point and the stopping point of a process, and it is important that this be decided upon by the group of people working on the process.

The second step is to define the boundaries of the process being mapped, determine the inputs and outputs, and from this define the first step and the last step of the process. The third step is to brainstorm within the group the activities and tasks that take place within the process. It is not necessary to try to move through the process logically at this stage. Brainstorming the tasks and putting them up on the storyboard is all that is required. The best way to do this is to use Post-It® notes or 3x5 cards to write the tasks and activities on and then stick them or pin them to a large piece of paper.

Once this is complete, then the team brings the tasks and activities into a logical sequence. It is useful to group the tasks into major activities and then to provide the links and sequence of the process map. This step can take considerable time because the people involved with development of the process map will often have different views of the same process and time will be needed for these people to talk through their various understandings and arrive at a consensus. Often additional analysis and information gathering is required before this consensus can be reached.

The last step is to draw the final version of the process map and review it with the other people in the company who are involved in this process so that they can validate the accuracy of the map.

The primary purpose of process mapping is for the team to gain an understanding of the processes they are studying and improving, and to provide a method of communicating this information to others. The goal is not to produce an artistic piece of work nor is it necessary to achieve it quickly. A good process map often takes a long time to develop because it includes the interaction of a group of experts, each of whom know one or two aspects of the process in detail, but need to learn from each other.

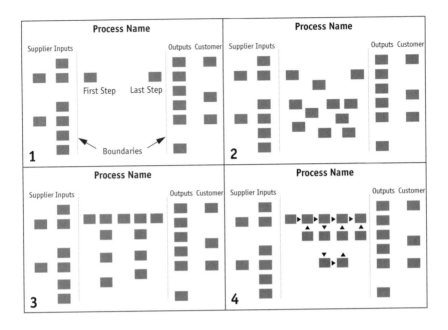

Figure 6-8. Storyboarding a Process Map

Analyzing a Process Map

Once the process map has been drawn it is often useful to analyze the steps within it. This analysis will vary according to the purpose of the project, but will often include the classification of each step using value-added codes. Another analysis is to calculate where the costs are being accrued, where quality problems are arising, and where delays occur. Useful factors are the value-added percentage (how much of the total time or cost is expended on value-added tasks) and the ratio of actual cycle time to theoretical cycle time.

Other times it is useful to present the map in a way that shows which departments are associated with each step in the process. A simplified example of this is shown in Figure 6-10.

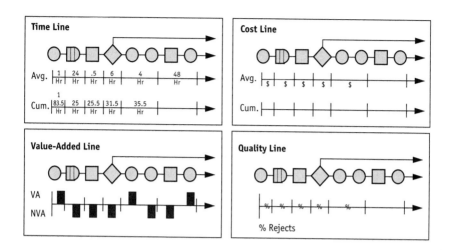

Figure 6-9. Process Maps with Analysis Data

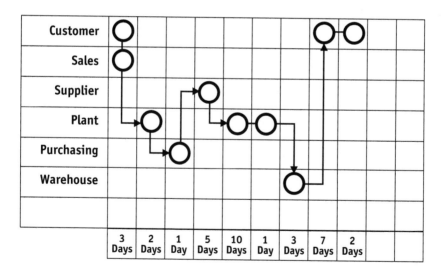

Figure 6-10. Process Map Showing Departments

Root Cause Analysis

It is important when creating improvement and reengineering within an organization to get to the root causes of problems. Many improvement projects have floundered because the people on the team have addressed the symptoms and not the root causes of the problems. Once a process map has been drawn and the analysis completed, it is important to analyze the problems and establish the root causes of the issues you are facing.

There are many techniques for establishing root cause, and they must be used appropriately; but the real issue is to spend the time as a team discussing and analyzing the issues, brainstorming the problems, and drilling down into the depth of the situation. Very often an improvement team will not take the time to do this. People complain about spending too much time in meetings. But the reality is that, in most companies, the issues and problems are deep seated and fundamental, and do not lend themselves to shallow analysis. Shallow analysis leads to shallow changes which lead to lack of benefit, and lost opportunity.

One technique for root cause analysis is the use of an affinity diagram, where the people in the team brainstorm the issues associated with a problem, using open-ended starting questions. The purpose is to bring out all the aspects of the problem in a free-form and open manner. Once the ideas are exhausted, then individuals within the team sort these ideas into groups. The grouping is done by several people in turn until the issues are brought into some clarity.

The power of an affinity diagram is that it gives the team the ability to get through to the essence of the problem and provides a foundation for breakthrough solutions.

Another important technique for getting to root causes is the use of matrix diagrams to relate different aspects of the issues together. The horizontal axis is used to divide the problem into logical pieces (for example, product families, kinds of customers, markets, kinds of quality problems) and the vertical axis lists the various issues that have been raised. The body of the matrix is used to mark comments and correlation information, to show the degree of cause and effect in each case, to mark the severity of the problem, and so forth.

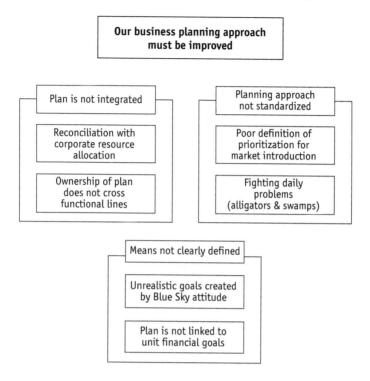

Figure 6-11. Simple Affinity Diagram

These diagrams are very helpful in clarifying and subdividing a series of problems so they can be better understood and resolved.

The classic method of establishing root causes is the *fishbone chart* or the *Ishikawa Diagram*. This method was devised by Kaoru Ishikawa, the Japanese quality expert, to provide a simple, effective visual tool for seeing cause and effect. An example of this chart is shown in Figure 6-12. The problem being studied is written at the end of the chart and the primary causes are shown on the first "bones" of the chart. The causes of these primary causes are shown going into the primary "bones," and the next level causes go into the next level "bones." This way the diagram builds up into an intricate network of causes.

When the team is developing a chart like this a large piece of paper is fixed to the wall, and Post-It® Notes are used to attach the causes as they are brought to light through brainstorming. If the primary causes are not easily understood then it is helpful to use some standard ones (*men, machines, materials,* and *methods*) as a starting point. They can be changed later as the exercise progresses.

The purpose with a cause and effect diagram is not to draw an elegant diagram but to uncover the true issues that cause the problems the team is trying to solve or improve.

Process Improvement and Reengineering

The primary purpose of a process improvement team is to change the process so that it is better aligned to company strategies and service to the customers, and to eliminate cost, reduce cycle time, and eliminate quality problems. These objectives require the team to work carefully to understand the process, establish the problems within it, understand the root causes of those problems, and create new processes that eliminate non-value-added tasks and activities, eliminate delays and waste, eradicate quality problems, and focus on company strategic goals and service to the customers.

The charts and methods described above are designed to enable the team to better understand the process (process maps), determine the problems and issues associated with the process (affinity diagram), analyze the root causes of the problems (matrices and fishbone charts), and analyze the cost, cycle time, and quality issues. A systematic method is required to help the team develop new approaches.

These new approaches may be improvements of the current process or they may be the development of entirely new, reengineered processes that are a radical departure for the company. Either way, a systematic method of assessing the problems and the potential for improvement is required.

A simple question matrix is helpful here (see Table 6-3) because it forces the team to ask the root questions of what, where, who, when, how, and a number of why's. Some Japanese quality experts advocate the use of "five why's" when analyzing an activity or a process for improvement purposes. The idea is that if you have

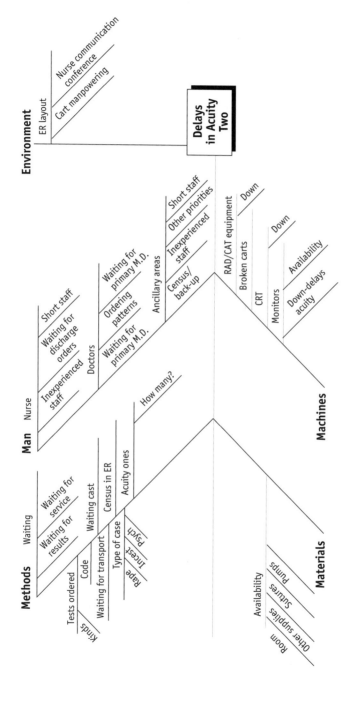

Figure 6-12. Fishbone Diagram of Possible Causes of Delays

asked "why" five times over, the team will have gotten to the root of the problem and will not be dealing with surface issues.

Table 6-3. Example of a Standard Question Matrix

Activity					
What is the purpose?	*Why* is it necessary?				
Where is it done?	*Why* is it done here?				
Who does it?	*Why* is it done by this person or machine?				
When is it done?	*Why* is it done then?				
How is it done?	*Why* is it this way?				

Table 6-4 is another set of standard questions that can be used to brainstorm and analyze each step in the process map, with a view to creating an entirely new and better approach.

Table 6-4. Another Example of Standard Questions

Can we:	Questions to ask:
• Eliminate non-value-added steps? • Perform steps in parallel? • Create a U-shaped layout? • Synchronize the steps? • Simplify the steps? • Eliminate unneeded motion? • Standardize performance? • Mistake proof the step (poka yoke)? • Eliminate transportation or material movement? • Prevent the problem through planned maintenance? • Eliminate unsafe operations?	• How is the customer (internal & external) effected by this? • How is the supplier (internal & external) effected by this? • Does this step require special training? • Does this step need documentation? • Is SPC applicable? • Are all factors known? • What are the potential problems in this step? • How can we eliminate the cause? • If we cannot eliminate the cause, how can it be minimized?

Summary

The improvement of business processes, both continuous improvement and radical reengineering, requires team-based and systematic methods of analyzing processes and creating improved methods. These analysis methods are valuable for activity-based management, target costing, value engineering, benchmarking, and other improvement methods.

Process mapping is a visual method for charting a business process so that it can be analyzed. Process mapping allows the internal knowledge of the company to be presented and communicated among team members and others. The process map is also a valuable tool for analyzing processes for improvement.

The idea of value-added analysis is to classify activities and tasks within a process to determine which are creating value in the eyes of the customer, and which are wasteful. Non-value-added activities need to be eliminated and value-added activities need to be improved by making them faster, less costly, and higher quality.

Real improvement can only come when the improvement team has established the root cause of the problems they are trying to solve. For an improvement project to be successful, it must be addressing and solving the root causes, not the symptoms. The techniques of affinity diagrams, cause and effect diagrams, and matrix analysis are useful for drilling down to the root causes.

Questions

1. What is a process?

2. Define the four different classifications of value-added and non-value-added.

3. What is the purpose of process mapping?

4. Would team-based storyboarding be useful in your company? What would be the benefits?

5. Which visual tools for root cause analysis would be most helpful to your organization? Where (which departments or processes) would you find them most useful?

7

Performance Measurement

Companies need a new approach to performance measurement. As they strive toward world class performance the traditional methods of measurement become a hindrance. New measures are needed.

Big changes are taking place in Western industry and these changes are happening fast. Traditional methods of measuring a company's performance no longer apply. They measure the wrong things and they mislead people. Issues important to world class companies include quality, productivity, on-time delivery, innovation, teamwork, flexibility, short cycle times, and closeness to customers. None of these issues are addressed by traditional management accounting measures.

As the needs and expectations of our customers change so must our measures, to ensure we are measuring the things our customers value. As management methods change and we move into teamwork approaches it is important to have measures that take the same approach. People are led and influenced by the way they are measured. If you measure the right things, people will do the right things. Traditional measures measure the *wrong things* for companies striving toward world class. New measures are needed that will lead people in the right direction.

Characteristics of the New Performance Measures

Many firms have begun to use new performance measures, in line with their world class approach. Most of these performance measures are not new ideas. Here is what is new. These measures truly drive the business, replace traditional cost accounting, and provide useful input at all levels of the company.

Every firm applies these ideas differently but common themes can be seen. Measures must:

- Relate directly to the business strategy
- Be primarily nonfinancial
- Vary between locations
- Change over time
- Be simple and easy to use
- Provide fast feedback of information
- Foster improvement rather than merely monitor it

Direct Relation to Business Strategy

World class companies have clear business strategies. The business strategy of a world class manufacturer focuses on issues like quality, reliability, short cycle times, flexibility, innovation, customer service, and environmental responsibility. Manufacturing strategy is one element of the company's business strategy, as is new product development and sales and marketing. Each strategy needs performance measures that directly address that strategy.

There are three reasons for keeping performance measures in line with the business strategy.

1. A company needs to know how well it is performing. Choose a few measures the managers can use to assess progress.
2. People focus on what you measure. If a firm measures and reports someone's work, the person will want to improve their

work. If the performance measures are directly related to the business strategy the people will be motivated toward the business strategy.

3. Measures provide feedback to help people and teams do their jobs and improve performance.

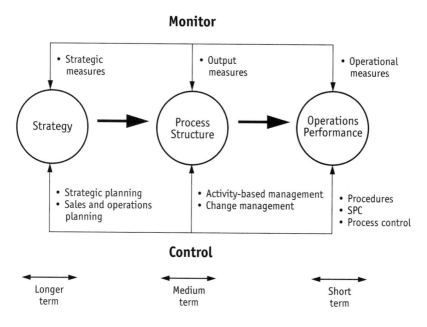

Figure 7-1. Links Between Strategies, Processes, and Operational Performance

Nonfinancial Measures

Traditional firms focus on financial results. World class companies stress nonfinancial measures. Accounting reports should not be used for performance measurement. They are not useful for daily control of the business. They are confusing and are often misleading.

For performance measures to be relevant, they must be expressed in terms that directly relate to the business strategy. To disguise the results in money terms is not helpful. Issues must be measured in terms that make direct sense to the people using them. If the measures are in dollars, the operations people must "translate" them into something real. If you want to improve quality, measure quality —not cost-of-quality. If you are concerned about cycle time, measure cycle time—not labor hour variances.

Variation Between Locations

The way firms apply world class manufacturing methods varies a lot. Each plant may be different. The products, customers, and employees may differ. Plants in different countries will certainly differ. A standard measurement method does not make sense.

Traditional companies use the same measures everywhere. They often pride themselves on being consistent and they often compare one plant against another. This is bad; teamwork is vital. You destroy the team when you judge one against the other. The trend of improvement is the real issue as people work in teams to improve the process. The teams will not work well together if they are rivals. Sharing information and ideas is positive; judging one against another is not.

To bring about major change you need a "champion," someone who leads the team to success. Two plants that are successful may have different champions with different ideas. The champions will do the job differently. Do not squash the champions by making them use standard measures which will not apply to both plants. You will measure the wrong things and also frustrate the champions.

Change Over Time

The measures need to change over time. Change is a key to a world class company. All world class firms value *continuous improvement*, a planned way for all employees to make their work increasingly better. Most changes are small, but when you put them together, they become a large step forward. When introducing world class methods, most companies start with a big improvement followed by a continuous improvement program.

Continuous improvement is not a catch phrase. It is a way of life within world class organizations. Continuous improvement means things change all the time. The performance measures must also change. When you start with world class methods some issues are more important than others. As time goes by the important issues will change. The measures must change to reflect this.

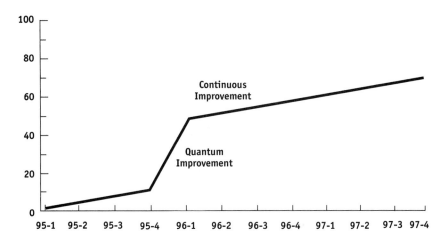

Figure 7-2. Improvement Measures

Simplicity and Ease of Use

For performance measures to work people must understand them. Complex measures do not work. Don't use ratios. Don't use measures combining many aspects into a single factor. These confuse people.

Plain and simple measures of the most important parts of the business are essential. Each issue must be measured directly and presented well. People then find the results easy to use and the measure is effective.

Performance measures within world class companies are clear and direct. Often these measures are made by people on the spot. They use wall charts, bulletin boards, graphs, signals, and computer screens. The best measures are the ones people make themselves. They understand them and trust the numbers. Even when measures are computer generated, analyzed, and consolidated they must still be straightforward and easy to use.

Fast Feedback of Information

Most companies get their measures monthly. They are accounting reports and follow the accounting calendar. They are often too late to be useful. There are often time-wasting meetings to "explain the variances." These meetings are to defend your actions, not improve performance.

A world class company fixes problems when they happen. It does not wait for month-end. The performance measures must help improve performance. To do this the information is needed fast, sometimes on the spot. Action cannot wait until the middle of next month. Quality, for example, cannot wait. Other information is needed twice daily, daily, or weekly. The feedback must match the need.

Fostering Improvement Rather Than Merely Monitoring

This last characteristic of performance measurement for a world class company has to do with motivation. Although this is intangible, it is of great importance. The performance measurement system will only work if the people using it find it helpful. It will not work if they feel they are being watched and judged.

Performance measures need to show clearly where improvement has been made and where more improvement is possible. Traditional measures are used to judge people. World class companies use measures to help people improve. This may sound like a subtle difference, but in practice it is the difference between success and failure.

Many of the issues already discussed have an impact on how the measures are used. On-time reports, easy-to-use charts and graphs, direct measurement, and measures that fit the firm's business strategy will help people focus on improvement.

Often measures are used to blame people or to assess their pay and promotion prospects. This creates fear. A world class company wants people to be creative, to try out new ideas, to take risks, ultimately to improve. Fear stops people from getting better. The measures must foster improvement.

Examples of New Performance Measures at Work

There are many approaches to performance measurement. The following examples show how some world class companies measure performance. However, every company must develop their own measures. There is no standard set.

Do not use too many measures. Companies often have too many measures. They work on the assumption that measuring many things creates more control. This is wrong. Too many measures create confusion and lack of focus. Pick six or eight measures that are sufficient to control your business and provide the balance of service, time, quality, and cost.

Delivery Performance and Customer Service

Everybody has customers. The customers may be the people using the products or services the company makes, or they may be other people within the organization. While the focus of customer service measures will be the ultimate customer who pays the invoices, even support departments (like a technical library for example) have customers within the organization. Measuring the customer's satisfaction is most important.

The best measure of customer satisfaction is direct feedback from the customers. Direct feedback can either be through surveys of the customers or by establishing automatic feedback like reply cards, questionnaires, or electronic data interchange (EDI). Reply cards and questionnaires are limited because only a few are returned. EDI receipt confirmation is more reliable and does not require additional data entry.

Often direct feedback is difficult to obtain and indirect measures like on-time shipments are used to track customer service levels. These measures show the amount of on-time deliveries and are usually presented as a graph. An average company will compare the date promised with the date shipped. A world class company will show the date the customer requested against the date shipped. The customer need is what is important—not what was promised.

Do not have many measures of customer service. Select one measure that addresses the customer's concerns and derive the company's customer service objectives from this one measure. Do not use measures that combine several factors because these confuse people and do not lead to improvement.

Process Time

A company's operation is, in fact, a series of processes performed repeatedly and these processes may span more than one department. Manufacturing processes are easily seen but service and support processes can be more difficult to define. Entering customer orders and meeting the customer needs is a process, as is providing accounting information and designing and enhancing products. All these process times can be measured.

Short process times are essential for world class companies. Short production process time results in low inventories. Short process times make a company more flexible to the customer's needs. Quick setups and changeovers are essential to short production process times.

World class companies stress timely service to customers, both internal and external. A simple measure is customer service time: the time from receipt of the order to dispatch of the product or service. This is a good measure of how quickly the customers are being served. It can often be measured directly from the company's computer systems for order entry and shipping.

Manufacturing process times can be measured, sampled, or derived. Most world class companies do not track a lot of detailed information about processes because it is wasteful. Do not introduce detailed tracking for performance measurement purposes only; it is non-value-added. Theoretical process times can be derived from production routings or process flow charts, if these documents are accurate and up-to-date.

Process times can be measured by sampling. For example, every hour on-the-hour everyone stops and measures their process time. Every 100th job is measured in detail. Every 10th kanban card is a different color and has space for entry of measurement information on the back of the card. This sample information is gathered, analyzed, and reported on a graph or chart.

Radical reductions in process time are achieved as companies introduce world class methods. A Department of Defense repair operation reduced their process time from 60 days to 8 days. A car seat manufacturer reduced customer lead times from 12 weeks to 90 minutes. The printed circuit board cell of an electronic equipment manufacturer reduced production cycle times from one and a half weeks to one day by introducing cellular manufacturing. These changes must be tracked and monitored.

Similarly, service and support processes can be measured: for example, the time to create invoices (shipment time to invoice being mailed or EDI'd), the time to retrieve and deliver a reference book from the technical library, the time to complete a month-end financial close, and the time to resolve customer service calls.

Innovation

In many industries, innovation is a key to the future. Product life cycles are getting shorter and the ability to introduce new products, new services, and new procedures is vital. A world class company stresses the need for every individual within the organization to be involved in improvement and innovation. It is not just new products that need to be innovative; new procedures and new services to the customers are also crucial.

How to measure new product innovation varies according to the company and the market. An organization that introduces many new products can continuously measure the rate of new product introduction or the number of new products per month or year. Companies that have fewer new products can measure the time-to-market of product. The time-to-market is defined as the time from conception of the product to its introduction to the marketplace. A Honda Motorcycle plant in Japan introduces one major product enhancement every month. The production process and working hours are geared around this need for new product introduction.

Another slant on innovation is the number of employee suggestions that are made and implemented. Many world class companies have clearly defined employee suggestion schemes. These methods keep careful track of who suggested what and how it was implemented. Companies that are advanced with these kinds of innovation methods often record the changes after they are made because the people are empowered to make the changes on their own authority. A good measure of suggestions is the number of suggestions per person per year or month. Toyota Motor Corporation is recorded to have achieved around 35 suggestions per person in one year. PSI Corporation in southern New Jersey is achieving 40 suggestions per person per year. Even though many of the suggestions are small, they add up to enormous improvement and very high employee involvement and commitment.

Productivity

The best way to measure productivity in a company or a plant is to measure directly the number of products or services provided per person. Ideally this should include everybody in the plant: the direct production people, the sales people, the engineers, the administrative people, and the managers. Often it is not possible to do this because these "indirect" people may work on products related to more than one plant, or they may be located in another facility and it is difficult to assign them to a specific product range. Most companies find that they can devise a sensible way of including a wide range of "direct" and "indirect" people into the calculation and make this a measure of the organization's overall effectiveness and productivity.

Sometimes it is not possible to use this measure because the company's product range includes widely different products, and the mix of products or services provided to customers often changes. Often this can be overcome by grouping the products into product families for reporting purposes and using simple, direct measures for each separate family.

Flexibility

Flexibility deals with the ability to make today what the customers want today and changing effectively as customer needs change. Traditional companies provide for customer needs by maintaining finished goods inventories and making-to-stock. World class companies build flexibility into their processes so they can make-to-order with very short lead times. Measures of flexibility are measures of the company's ability to meet this demand. Flexibility can be measured through such issues as the level of cross-training in the plant, the cycle time from placing an order to shipping the goods, the degree of commonality of component parts throughout the products, the degree of common processes across the production floor, the modularity of the product design, the position of variability within the products, and so forth.

Quality

To say that quality is an important aspect of world class manufacturing is an understatement. Some companies would say that quality *is* world class manufacturing—that everything else stems from a long-term commitment to improving quality.

Measurement of quality can start with the suppliers. Measuring the quality of incoming material enables you to create reports of vendor quality. However, a world class company will not want to be doing a lot of incoming inspection of components and raw material because this is a non-value-added activity. The objective is to certify individual suppliers to provide components and raw materials that are up to standard and on time. A measure of the percentage of suppliers certified or the percentage of materials provided by certified suppliers is often helpful.

Production quality is almost always measured in terms of rejects per thousand or rejects per million items. This is a straightforward, easy to understand method of measuring quality. Another approach is to measure the number of processes using statistical process control (SPC) and the number of those processes that are "under control."

Customer satisfaction is another good measure of quality. It measures not only the quality of the product but the quality of the service the customer is receiving. Customer satisfaction is best measured by direct feedback from customer surveys. A company with many customers may need to survey a sample number; others can survey all the customers. The key to surveys is to be brief, focused, and addressed to the right people. Some companies use Snake Charts (see Figure 7-3) because they show not only the customers' opinions of service received, but also the importance they place on each aspect of the service. We may be doing a great job and score very highly on issues the customers consider to be unimportant, while scoring poorly on other aspects the customers consider to be of higher significance.

Other quality issues that should be measured involve the accuracy of information within the computer system. You cannot be a world class manufacturer and maintain high levels of product quality if your information is poor. Primary issues are accuracy in inventory, forecast, bill of materials, and production routing. These issues can be measured as a part of the company's information accuracy maintenance processes like cycle counting and engineering change processing.

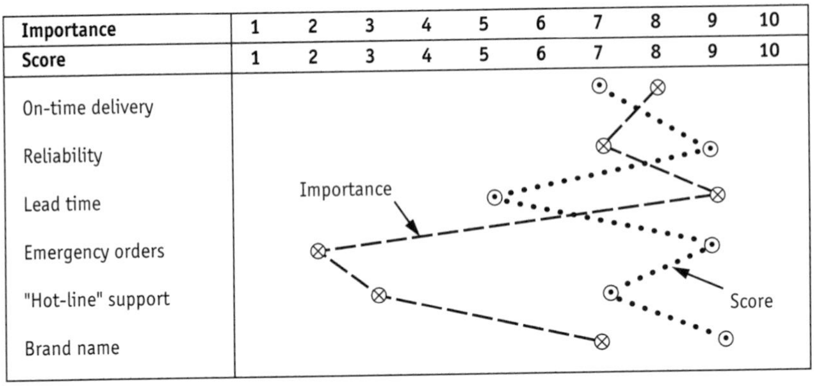

Importance	1	2	3	4	5	6	7	8	9	10
Score	1	2	3	4	5	6	7	8	9	10

On-time delivery

Reliability

Lead time

Emergency orders

"Hot-line" support

Brand name

Figure 7-3. Customer Service Snake Chart

Financial Performance Measures

While nonfinancial performance measures are better than financial measures, there *are* some legitimate reasons for using financial measures. The primary reason for using a financial measure is if there is a need for a "common denominator" to consolidate dissimilar information on a single report. There are two cautions when using financial performance measures.

The first is that the definition of the financial information needs to be determined carefully. Often, standard costs, sales figures, market value, and the like are used to present the information which can be quite misleading.

The second caution is that many companies use financial reports to make comparisons between plants, locations, and departments. These comparisons are not compatible with a world class approach where teamwork and continuous improvement are emphasized. Teamwork breaks down when judgmental comparisons are made between plants or departments. Similarly, the issue is not the actual value of the measure, but the way it is changing over time. If you are using financial measures so that comparisons can be made, stop it and develop nonfinancial measures that are appropriate to the different needs of the locations.

Performance measures can be shown in financial terms when a "common denominator" is required to summarize heterogeneous data such as the scrap value of a wide variety of components or products (see Figure 7-4). Useful financial measures are such things as scrap reporting, inventory turns derived from financial information, value-added ratios derived from activity-based analysis, and product costs and profitabilities.

Social Issues

Everybody recognizes that the issues of teamwork, morale, leadership, and participation are of crucial importance to a world class company yet these issues are difficult to measure. Traditional measures make no attempt to address these issues and focus on the "bottom line." There are, however, a number of approaches that companies use to try to gauge their success in these areas.

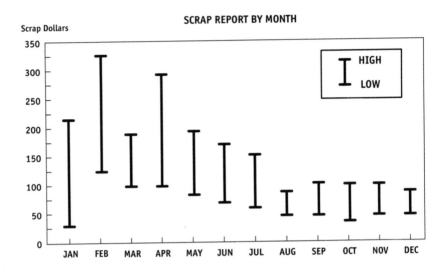

Figure 7-4. Scrap Reporting Using "Upper and Lower" Charts

Morale and teamwork can be measured using the time-honored negative measures of employee turnover, productive days lost through absenteeism, etc. More positive measures of morale and teamwork can be derived from direct measures of people's involvement in participation activities. The percentage of people on participation teams (providing these teams are voluntary), the number of suggestions per person, the number of suggestions implemented, the amount of education or training classes taken per person, and the average number of certified skills per person within the plant or office are also good measures.

Leadership can be measured using personnel surveys and work environment measures. These measures vary from highly complex sociological surveys to straightforward questionnaires. One of the complex measures is the Stanford Work Environment Scale that uses three questionnaires to measure such issues as involvement, peer cohesion, and autonomy. Simpler forms have been devised by such organizations as Kodak and the Federal Census Bureau. These forms ask straightforward questions like "Does your manager provide you with adequate training?" and "Do you feel part of a team in your department?"

World class companies tend to be very concerned about safety and environmental issues. They often establish safety and environmental audits within the organization. These audits are typically more stringent than government regulations and are conducted on a regular basis throughout the organization. Reports are made to show the degree to which each department or area is adhering to the company's safety and environmental code.

Implementing New Performance Measurements

A new measurement system is a major change and must be introduced with great care. Do not be tempted to do a "quick and dirty" implementation. Changing measures changes the way people work. What you measure is what you get.

There are eight steps required to establish a new approach to performance measurement:

1. Establish a clear understanding of the strategic issues.
2. Set goals and objectives for each strategic area.
3. List the critical success factors (CSFs) required to achieve the strategic issues.
4. Validate the critical success factors.
5. Link the critical success factors to the company's primary processes.
6. Develop key measures for each critical success factor.
7. Use the measures in a "pilot" area.
8. Expand the measures to the whole plant or company.

Step One: Write a Strategy

The starting point for the development of new performance measures is a clear understanding of the company's strategies. A common mistake when developing new performance measures is to jump too quickly to the development of measures. Understanding the company's strategies is a foundation for developing strategically-based performance measures.

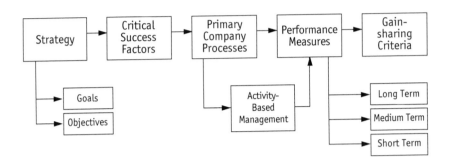

Figure 7-5. Development of Strategy-Based Performance Measures

Step Two: Set Goals and Objectives for Each Strategic Issue

Defining strategic issues is helpful for clarifying where the company needs to go, but it is necessary to also develop goals and objectives for these strategies to become reality. The next step is to establish, through the company's senior managers, the goals and objectives for each strategic issue. A strategy is just a good idea if it has no clearly defined goals and no plan to achieve them. Objectives state the *qualitative* direction in which the company wishes to go, and the goals state the *quantitative* outworking of those objectives.

Spend the time to get these goals and objectives right. Often the team will be treading on politically dangerous ground. It is better to stir up the political ambiguities of the organization at this stage than to continue to pretend. A world class or agile company will be very concerned to match reality to rhetoric.

Step Three: List the Critical Success Factors

Once a strategy is written, the critical success factors (CSFs) can be defined. The CSFs are the actions by the company that make the strategy real. The strategy is the path to success. The CSFs are the stepping stones on the path.

Make a list of what must be done to put the strategy into action. Review it carefully with the people responsible for making things happen. Managers, shopfloor people, office workers, and people in the field all need to be included. There needs to be a clarity of understanding within the company so that everybody is moving in the same direction and understands why. The new performance measures must augment the company's strategic direction, and can do so only if the CSFs are clearly understood.

Step Four: Validate the Critical Success Factors

Stating critical success factors does not mean that the company is serious about implementing them. Having established the critical success factors linked to each strategy it is important to validate to what extent these CSFs are being applied within the company. Make a list of the actions the company *has taken* to make each strategic improvement a reality.

Many companies pay lip service to such issues as serving the customer, providing high quality, and achieving world class service. Only tangible actions make a strategy real. Check that you are really taking steps to bring the strategy to life before building a performance measurement program.

Step Five: Link the CSFs to Primary Processes

All company activities are processes and it is important to understand which processes affect the CSFs of the business, because these are the processes that need to be understood and improved. Once the CSFs have been understood and agreed upon by the people involved, then the team needs to establish a list of the processes that make up the CSFs.

There are hosts of processes associated with a company and some pragmatism is required to define the *primary* processes. It can be difficult to determine where one process begins and another process ends. A good rule of thumb is to establish approximately 15 processes for the company. Only select processes that have some bearing on the CSFs; the other processes are, by definition, unimportant for the purposes of performance measurement development. Activity-based management will generate output measures for each process and activity within a process. This analysis is often valuable when developing performance measures that augment process improvement initiatives.

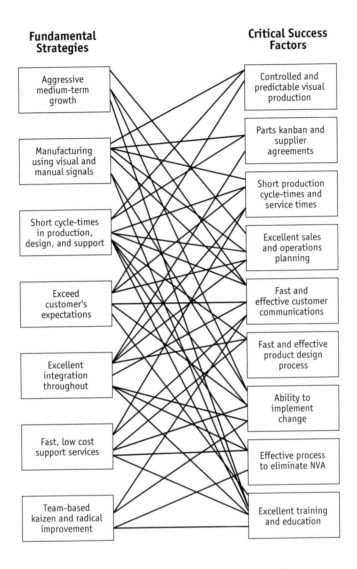

Fundamental Strategies

- Aggressive medium-term growth
- Manufacturing using visual and manual signals
- Short cycle-times in production, design, and support
- Exceed customer's expectations
- Excellent integration throughout
- Fast, low cost support services
- Team-based kaizen and radical improvement

Critical Success Factors

- Controlled and predictable visual production
- Parts kanban and supplier agreements
- Short production cycle-times and service times
- Excellent sales and operations planning
- Fast and effective customer communications
- Fast and effective product design process
- Ability to implement change
- Effective process to eliminate NVA
- Excellent training and education

Figure 7-6. Pictorial View of Strategies Linked to CSFs

Step Six: Develop Key Measures

Once the strategy is well understood and validated, the CSFs are established, and the processes supporting the CSF's are understood, you are ready to start developing new measures.

In general, a company requires three levels of performance measures: operational measures, process measures and strategic measures. The operational measures measure day-to-day on the shop floor or warehouse, in the offices, and out in the field. They are taken frequently by the people doing the job. The process measures control the processes that provide success in the company's objectives. These are more cumulative and taken perhaps weekly primarily for the process owners. The strategic measures track and control the company's success at putting the strategies into action, and are taken less frequently for use by the senior managers.

Every measure must meet the seven criteria discussed previously in this chapter. Link each measure to a CSF. Think about the format for reporting the measure. Where will the data come from? How easy to gather the data? What makes this a good measure? What are the weaknesses of the measure? Can the measure be consolidated across departments or cells?

The best measures are reported directly by the people using them, and use data that is already available for other reasons. Some companies make that a rule. It is wasteful to gather data for performance measurement alone.

The best measures are presented graphically. Pictures are better than words or numbers. Plan the format carefully. Can the people using the measures draw their own charts? Are the measures flexible enough to meet the needs of each cell or department? Do you need different measures for each cell or department?

Some companies focus on presentation. They do not specify how the measures should be calculated, just how they should be presented. For example, every department must report their quality, throughput time, cost, and customer service. The results must be shown on four graphs presented on a single sheet of paper. Each cell or department devises their own measures but they present them in the same format. By the same token, if consolidation is important it is best to gather and report the measured data through a computer system.

Step Seven: Pilot the New Performance Measures

As with most significant changes, it is best to try it out before committing to it. Start using the new performance measures in a pilot area of the company. Select a self-contained part of the business, develop the measures and put them into practice. The pilot will reveal any shortcoming, as well as showing how a new approach to measurement is helpful.

Step Eight: Expand the Measures to the Whole Plant or Company

Once the pilot has shown that the new measures work well, expand them to the entire plant. This will require abandoning the old measures. This is where the "rubber meets the road." It takes courage to abandon the old measures, but it must be done. You cannot have two performance measurement systems running at the same time.

Make sure the people using the new measures have been trained. It is important to show people why the new measures are better. If the new measures present a bigger challenge, you will have to provide more training and more education. Have the team people available for informal training and encouragement.

Summary

New performance measures are required when a company moves from traditional approaches into *world class* methods. The old approach was heavily biased towards financial measures and did not focus on the *real* issues that create value and service to the customers and wealth to the company. Frequently the traditional measures focused on issues that made people do things that were positively harmful to the business.

A new approach to performance measures requires understanding the company's business strategies and the CSFs that can make the strategy a reality. From this understanding a team-based performance measurement development project can be initiated. The new measures will be strategically based, primarily nonfinancial, and can change over time and from one part of the company to another. They will be easy to use, provide fast and effective feedback, and will foster improvement rather than merely monitor the business.

The development of these kinds of performance measures starts with studying the company's strategies and understanding the CSFs of the organization. These CSFs are linked to the company's primary business processes, and goals and objectives are established. This analysis is difficult to do and requires the liaison and cooperation of many people throughout the company. It is essential that this process is real and not just "window dressing."

The easiest part of the process is the development of the performance measures themselves. Once the analysis has been done thoroughly the performance measures fall out readily. The new measures must adhere to the seven criteria given above.

Questions

1. Are the performance measures used by your company directly linked to the company's strategies?

2. List the company's primary strategies and think through which critical success factors affect these strategies most profoundly.

3. Do your current measures adhere to the seven criteria for performance measurement presented in this chapter?

4. Can you control your company's production area with six or fewer measures? What would they be?

Interlude

Bean Counters No More

Bean Counters No More[†] was the theme of a recent edition of *Management Accounting* magazine, the journal of the Institute of Management Accountants in Montvale, NJ. Most of the magazine was dedicated to case studies of companies where the accounting people had shed the old image of the green eyeshade accountant laboring in a back room to produce irrelevant, incomprehensible, and late reports. These accountants had made the transition to 'agents of change'.

Technical Editor Susan Jayson noted that "the number one complaint of management accountants with ten years or more experience is that 'management doesn't listen to us. We have a lot of knowledge about the company, but when it comes to key business decisions, we are not in the loop. We are thought of as bean counters. Given the chance, we could really add value.'"

[†] Extracts used by permission of the Institute of Management Accountants, Montvale, New Jersey.

South Central Bell

Steven Harrison, manager of regulatory accounting at South Central Bell says "we were able to shed our scorekeeper image forever by showing how accountants can be value-added business partners and an integral part of the management team. To do this, we had to step out of the traditional role of compilers, and take on the roles of interpreter, advisor, and partner."

In his article "Not Just Bean Counters," Mr. Harrison goes on to relate the story of how deregulation in the telephone industry threw South Central Bell into a reporting nightmare. The old reporting systems were disbanded with the demise of "Ma Bell" and there was no agreement among the managers of the new company. There was a sharp and partisan conflict. It was decided that the accountants should take a proactive role.

During the next year, employees from the comptroller's department attended staff meetings with employees from the marketing and network departments. At some meetings they gave presentations. At other sessions they just listened—but were there. Thus the accountants learned about the concerns of the marketing manager and saw the difficulties caused by some of their existing policies and procedures.

They spent weeks with the marketing and network employees examining in great detail the cost allocation process. This exchange gave marketing and network employees a much better understanding of the accounting processes, and gave our accountants a much more complete understanding of the field operations and a chance to see parts of the business they normally did not run into.

In one state, a comptroller department employee was transferred to the network department to lend financial expertise. In another state a comptroller department person was moved into the marketing department. In yet another state, at the annual marketing awards banquet, a member of the comptroller's department was awarded a "Spirit of Service" award to recognize his contribution. He was the first accountant to be awarded this prize.

Automatic Feed Company

"The key is convincing managers we can solve more problems than we create!" states Nathan Weaks, treasurer of Automatic Feed Company. "Unfortunately," he adds, "accountants tend to get absorbed in financial reporting. They are more concerned with meeting the needs of outsiders. Consequently, the accountant's inside customers, who are critical to his or her advancement, get little direct benefit."

Automatic Feed Company was facing enormous problems with scheduling production. This came to a head when their largest customer threatened to cancel the company's largest ever order if they did not start delivering on time. This crisis gave rise to an opportunity for the company's newly appointed treasurer to show that an accountant can be an agent of change.

To the astonishment and amazement of his colleagues in operations, marketing, and engineering, the treasurer quickly analyzed the situation and was able to develop an innovative and challenging solution to this chronic and damaging problem. The solution was not an easy one; it broke the paradigms and trod on a few toes. And many people were taken aback when the president assigned the treasurer to head up the team that was to implement the new scheduling system.

Using a four step, team-based approach, Mr. Weaks studied the problem in detail, defined the new approach, applied simplifying procedures, piloted the methodology, and implemented the new system in about six months. The new approach was simple, proven, low cost (less than $10,000 of software development), and very effective.

The company's ability to keep promises and deliver on time was a major contributing factor to the doubling of annual sales, and the new scheduling system has been an important tool for identifying bottlenecks to company growth. In addition, when large projects are involved, the output reports from the scheduling system are automatically sent to customers because they have proven to be valuable customer communication tools.

Mr. Weaks concludes, "Traditionally in Automatic Feed's engineering-manufacturing environment the accounting function has been a second-class citizen. But solving the scheduling problem has solved that mentality. Scheduling has enabled our accountants to become more knowledgeable about our products—especially the products of design and manufacture. As managers came to trust and use the information provided by the scheduling system, the accountants have become accepted members of the management team."

8

A New Approach to Product Design

In recent years forward-thinking companies have been approaching product design in a very different way. These approaches vary from company to company, but can be grouped under the heading of concurrent engineering. The objectives of concurrent engineering include:

- Reduced design time
- Improved product quality
- Improved profitability by reducing design costs, manufacturing costs and product life cycle costs
- Design for ease of manufacture
- Meeting or exceeding customer requirements and expectations

We must get better at designing products if we are to be competitive. There are some clear trends emerging including product proliferation, short time-to-market, and mass customization.

Product Proliferation

There are many more products being introduced now than in previous years. In 1981 2,689 new consumer products were introduced to grocery and drug stores in the United States. In 1991 this figure rose to 16,143 products. A new product was introduced every half-hour that year. Yet David Glass, CEO of Wal-Mart, complained that "there was an absolute dearth of new and exciting fashion-forward products" (Peters 1994). More and more new products are being introduced faster and faster—but our customers still want more.

Time-to-Market

It used to take Chrysler Corporation about eight years to design a new car from concept to showroom. This was standard for the industry. The innovative Chrysler Concorde range of cars was designed from scratch and took less than 39 months. This matches the design cycle of Nissan, Toyota, and other world class companies.

In some industries, for example consumer electronics, it is vital to be first to market with a new product idea. Profitability is to a large extent dependent upon being first in the marketplace. Quality is important, good design is important, good marketing and customer support processes are important. But profitability over the product's life cycle is significantly affected by when you enter the market.

Mass Customization

Consumer goods manufacturers used to have a focused range of products that were sold through retailers to the public. These days the major retailers want their own custom products, and not just self-labeled products, but products with different features and functions that meet the needs of their target customers.

Similarly, suppliers in every kind of industry are finding that their customers increasingly require small quantities of customized products instead of buying "standard" items. This trend towards customized products (and the agile manufacturing methods required to meet it) is a major change taking place in Western manufacturing. The term mass customization has been coined to describe this trend (Pine 1993).

What Is Wrong with the Traditional Design Approach?

The traditional approach to design takes too long and is too expensive. It requires considerable redesign at each stage, relies on pilot production to "iron out" the problems, and is often not customer focused.

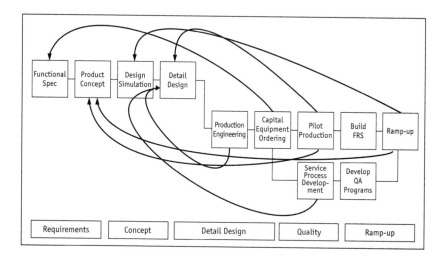

Figure 8-1. Traditional "Over the Fence" Design

Figure 8-1 shows a typical traditional design process, sometimes called "over the fence design" because each department works separately and then throws the design over the fence to the next department. Traditional design processes take a long time because the work is done sequentially—one department followed by the next, followed by the next.

The traditional approach is:

- Too long because it takes a long time to process the design through each department and to complete the reviews and redesigns required.
- Too expensive because there are many redesign activities as shortcomings of the original design are identified later by other departments. This results in many changes taking place later in

the process. Changes are more complex and expensive when they are made later in the design process.

- Likely to produce a poorer quality product because the needs of the customers, the manufacturing process, the customer service department, and the quality assurance people are not taken into account in the early stages of design. These needs are patched in later in the process and inevitably lead to a less satisfactory result.

Concurrent Engineering

- Shortening Lead Times

- Raising Quality

Concurrent Engineering

Concurrent engineering (also called simultaneous or parallel engineering) seeks to eliminate the problems of traditional design by having all the departments work together as a team to design a new product. This approach is faster because the development tasks are done in parallel and much of the waiting and paper shuffling is eliminated.

Concurrent engineering also results in better designs because the early design work takes account of the needs of production, quality, marketing, customer service, and other areas critical to the product's success. It is possible to design the product for ease of manufacture, to design high quality into the product, to make the product easier to support after the sale. If these issues are addressed in the functional and conceptual stages of the design the result is a better product.

Concurrent engineering also reduces the cost of developing a new product. Figure 8-2 shows a typical pattern of development costs.

Despite the largest costs being incurred later in the design process, the majority of costs are *committed* in the early stages. Concurrent engineering seeks to minimize these costs by having a wide range of people contribute to these decisions in the early stages.

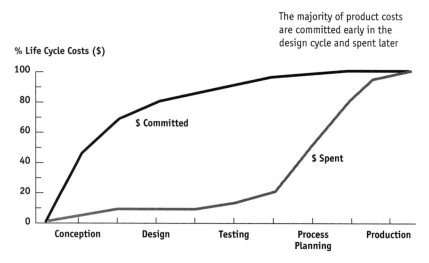

Figure 8-2. Life Cycle Time and Costs

The elimination of pilot production is an important objective of concurrent engineering. If a company is introducing new products much more quickly it cannot afford the time and disruption it takes to do pilots. To eliminate pilots the design must be done "right first time." The quality, production, marketing, and customer service issues must be dealt with up front so that the design is right *before* the product goes into production.

Figure 8-3 shows the spread of engineering changes with a concurrent engineering approach. Instead of many ECNs being applied after production has started (the most complex and expensive time to do engineering changes), the emphasis is on getting all the design changes done early in the process.

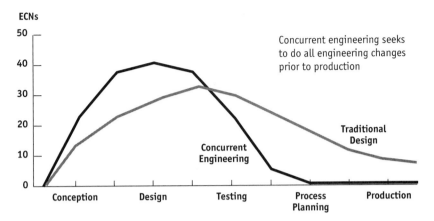

Figure 8-3. Engineering Changes During Design

Methods of Concurrent Engineering

Concurrent engineering is not easy. It requires excellent project planning and management skills. It requires good cooperation between the various departments of the company. It requires teamwork, attention to detail, vision, commitment, and very high standards (see Hartley 1992). These are all attributes that differentiate world class companies.

Some of the keys to success are:

- *Cross-functional teams*
  Concurrent engineering requires teams of people from different disciplines working together. Each person brings their own specialty but they are also part of the team and are involved with activities outside of their own specific responsibilities. Often customers and suppliers are included in these teams. The management accountant has a vital role to play in a concurrent design team.

- *Integrated approach*
  This is the opposite of the "over the fence" method. The project is organized so that each aspect of the design can be achieved concurrently. Everyone is involved with bringing the

product to market quickly and perfectly. This requires excellent integration of the work. There is no less work to do; it must be integrated into a tight schedule.

- *Detailed analysis*
  There is no substitute for doing all the homework. One reason traditional companies use pilots to highlight problems is that their design process does not look at the issues in enough detail. Part of the concept of total quality management is paying very close attention to what causes problems and solving these root causes. This must be the approach to concurrent engineering if the design is to be "right first time."

- *Customer focused design*
  A major benefit of concurrent engineering is that the cross-functional team has the people required to handle all the important aspects of the design. Successful concurrent engineering teams focus on the needs of the customer. The customer has quality needs, feature and function needs, and price needs. The price is almost always driven by the needs of the customer.

- *Tough-to-reach targets*
  Concurrent engineering teams usually set themselves tough targets. These targets include cost targets, quality targets, time-to-market targets, and product functional targets. The targets are set early in the process and then refined as the design takes shape. The accountants are involved in target setting tasks.

The benefits of a concurrent engineering approach reach to every part of the company:

- Increased customer satisfaction
- Increased market share
- Faster time-to-market
- Few engineering changes
- Reduced total lifetime costs
- Reduced design costs
- Reduced manufacturing costs

- Reduced warranty costs
- Improved communications within the company
- Improved cooperation with suppliers

Role of the Accountant in Product Design

There are exciting new roles for accountants as their companies move into new product design methods like concurrent engineering. There are new techniques to be learned and used. These include:

- Target costing
- Value engineering
- Life cycle costing
- Quality function deployment
- Variety effectiveness analysis
- Continuous improvement

As well as applying these techniques, the accountants also make a contribution as a team member. The analytical skills of accountants lend themselves well to product design teams. This is the strength of a cross-functional team. People from different disciplines bring their own perspectives to the task. This creative synergy of a diverse group is powerful, and is one of the reasons concurrent engineering teams create better designs.

Target Costing

Target costing starts with an understanding of the market. The target costs for a new product are derived from the price the customers are willing to pay for the product. Accountants work with sales and marketing to understand the parameters of the market and make a judgment about the price the market will bear. If the new product is a variation of a current product then the market price may be assessed quite easily. If the product is entirely new it is more difficult to determine the market price.

The company will have established a policy of how much gross profit they wish to make on a product. By subtracting the target profit from the sales price, the allowable cost can be calculated. The allowable cost is the product cost required to achieve the target profit the company wishes to make.

Target Costing

- Used in product planning and design

- Involves cost planning, *not* cost control

- Matches product costs to customer needs and company needs prior to production

- Used for product costs, R&D costs, and post-production usage costs

---

Based on the current design of the new product, which may be very early in the design process, the current estimated cost can be determined. Early in the process these estimated costs may be unreliable. As the design progresses the estimated costs will become firmer figures. The difference between the allowable cost and the estimated cost is called the *cost gap*. During the design process this cost gap must be bridged if the company is to achieve the desired profit. The role of the accountant on the team is to work with the engineers and other team members to achieve the allowable cost.

In practice the allowable cost is often far less than the current estimated cost. To establish the allowable cost as a goal in the early stages of the design would be to set an unattainable objective that would not serve a useful purpose. The accountants establish *target costs* for the product or for major subassemblies of the product. The target costs must be within reach of the team but must also be aggressive goals.

Early in the design process the target costs will be established for the product and for major pieces of the product. For example, there will be a target cost for an automobile model made up of the targets for the body, the transmission, the motor, and other major subassemblies. Later in the design process the target costs will be applied to a lower level and include components and smaller subassemblies. It is often not necessary to establish targets for every part. The level of target costing is a judgment that must be made by the team.

The targets themselves also change over time. The purpose of the targets is to provide the design team with a tough but attainable cost goal. The team uses design techniques and value engineering analysis to bring the estimated cost in line with the target. As soon as you attain the target, the target is moved. Once the team has built the target costs into the product design, the accountants (in liaison with the rest of the team) establish a more aggressive set of targets. This procedure is repeated throughout the design processes until the estimated cost is brought into line with the allowable cost. The company's profit goals can then be satisfied.

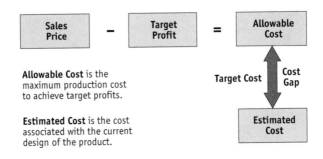

Target Cost will be attainable,
but only with considerable effort.

Figure 8-4. The Target Cost Calculation

Target costing (Monden 1992; Sakurai 1992) is a systematic method for establishing motivating goals for the team that are tough yet attainable, and are based on real data developed within the team. These targets are not set by outsiders. They are set by the team members themselves who are then committed to their successful achievement. The accountants on the team not only establish the target costs but are responsible, as team members, to make them a reality.

Target costing is not used solely for product costing. Targets are also set for the cost of the design process itself, post-production issues like distribution costs, and sometimes for the usage and disposal costs that are incurred by the customer. This way the team is able to keep focused on the needs of the customer and the larger needs of the organization. A recent survey of Japanese companies using target costing showed that less than half the target costs related to the product costs themselves. Other target costs related to the design, distribution, and use of the products.

Value Engineering

Value engineering is a set of formal techniques used to bring the design into line with the target costs. Value engineering is a planned and orderly approach to the assessment of product costs throughout the design process. The formal definition of value engineering is an activity to design a product from many different angles, to meet the customer's needs, to meet the organization's objectives, at the lowest possible cost.

The processes and procedures of value engineering vary considerably from one organization to another according to the products being designed and the needs of the market. But the essential elements are that the design engineers, production engineers, field service engineers (if necessary), purchasing people, suppliers, and accountants work together in a team to eliminate cost from the design of the product or segments of the product. This is done through careful analysis of what drives the costs, innovative engineering (both design and process), and cooperative material sourcing.

Value Engineering

The systematic, team-based method used to bring actual costs into line with target costs.

In the early stages of a product design the target costs will be established at a macro level. The finished product will be broken down into its major assemblies and a target cost established for each major assembly. Value engineering methods will be used to bring the cost of the major assemblies into line with the target before the detailed design is started. As the design progresses and the individual component parts and their production processes are designed, value engineering is used to optimize the costs of each lower-level part and subassembly.

- Make Estimated Cost = Target Cost
- Team approach to planned cost reduction
- Used at initial stage, detailed design, and after production begins

A Planned and Orderly Approach

- Does not trade off quality for cost
- Encourages creativity and innovation
- Companywide approach

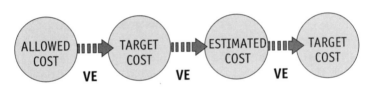

Figure 8-5. How Value Engineering Works

An important skill required of the accountant in this process is the ability to create accurate estimated costs throughout the design process. These costs cannot be "rolled up" in the traditional way because the product has not yet been fully designed. The accountant must use analogy with other similar products, heuristic cost forecast methods, and educated guesses throughout this process. It is imperative that the accounting people involved with value engineering have a good understanding of the engineering associated with the product design. They must understand the production processes, the characteristics of the materials being used, the software, machine tools, jigs, fixtures, etc. It is not necessary for the accountants to become engineering experts, but they must have a good understanding of the products and processes they are working on.

Life Cycle Costing

The purpose of life cycle costing during product design is to provide a broader view of the product costs being calculated. As product ranges increase and the life cycle of individual products gets shorter it becomes more important to understand the costs of designing, developing, manufacturing, and distributing product families rather than individual products. Similarly, as products become increasingly complex and the technology costs increase, it becomes important to understand the total costs of a product over its entire life cycle instead of just knowing the immediate production costs.

Life Cycle Costing

• Provides a long-term perspective for product design.

• Makes for better strategic decision making.

• Maximizes profits over the product's lifetime.

Life cycle costing has been important in some industries for many years. Pharmaceutical manufacturers, for example, have enormous research and development costs that frequently produce no direct results at all. The development costs of new pharmaceuticals are very high and can encompass many years of work. These costs must be understood in light of the costs and revenues of the products over their entire lifetime, and in the many marketing forms the product takes.

Marketing people are concerned with lifetime costs. The launch of a new product or product family is often preceded by an analysis of the expected revenues and costs over the number of years the product is expected to be sold. Marketing plans and approaches require a long-term view.

The ultimate goal of life cycle costing is to enable the designers, engineers, manufacturers, marketers, and company executives to make decisions that will maximize the profit made from a product (or product family) over the lifetime of the product. Life cycle costing affects many aspects of strategic decision making including pricing, profit objectives, product development plans, and product retirement plans.

Life cycle costing also relates the new product or product family to a broader organizational perspective. The marketers, designers, engineers, and manufacturing people involved with the project can see the new product in the context of the company's product range and corporate aspirations.

Figure 8-6 shows the four stages of a product's life cycle: startup, growth, maturity, and decline. The costs associated with each stage are significantly different and it is important for the accountant to have an understanding of how these costs change over time.

Better decisions can be made when the life cycle costs and profitabilities are understood. A product's location within its life cycle can impact decisions associated with product differentiation, pricing, risk assessment, market entry, market share, marketing strategy, production volumes, product performance, and product abandonment.

	STARTUP	GROWTH	MATURITY	DECLINE
Objective	Sales Growth	Sales Growth	Profits	Cash Flow/Profits
Perf. Measure	Quality Service	Quality Service	Price	Price
Product R & D	High	Moderate	Moderate	Low
Process R & D	Moderate	High	High	Low
Advertising	Moderate	High	Moderate	Low
Plant and Equipment	Low	High	Moderate	Low

Figure 8-6. Aspects of the Life Cycle

Including Usage Costs in Life Cycle Costing

Some companies examine product life cycle costs from the company's perspective and from the customer's perspective. The company is concerned with profitability over the life cycle of the product. The customer is concerned with the product's performance at a given price. The customer is also concerned with the cost of using the product. The product may require maintenance or repair, it may need special installation, it may need fuel or other items added to it, and there may be a cost of finally disposing of the product. To fully understand the product's place in the market and its overall cost and profitability, the company must understand the life cycle costs from the customer's perspective as well.

For instance, the public is increasingly concerned about environmental and ecological issues. Companies concerned to understand the lifetime profitability of their products are taking life cycle costing a step further by including societal costs into their cost models. This approach is currently in its early stages but there is every sign that government and other institutions will be requiring a more comprehensive view of the cost and benefits of a product. If, for example, every company was required, at its own expense, to dispose of its products after the customer had finished using them, this would have a significant impact on the design and promotion of the company's products. Some of the more progressive companies are using life cycle costing to assess these issues today so they can be a step ahead of this trend.

Calculating Life Cycle Costs

The big problem with life cycle costing in the design stages of a product is that it is very difficult to determine the costs and revenues of a product over its life cycle. Like any forecast, life cycle costs are always wrong. Sometimes they are very wrong. This should not deter us from calculating these costs because the accuracy will improve over time.

The first step towards developing a lifetime cost model is to do a detailed breakdown of the cost contributors. This is where life cycle costing integrates with target costing and activity-based costing.

Many of the cost contributors required for life cycle costing fore-casts will have already been identified as a part of the target costing analysis. Similarly, as the target costing activities become more detailed and precise throughout the design process, so the life cycle cost forecasts can develop in scope and detail.

It is important when developing a life cycle cost model to have a thorough understanding of the market. This is where the accoun-tants will work with the sales and marketing personnel to determine where the product fits in the marketplace, what this product brings that differentiates it from other similar products, and what the cus-tomer's patterns of purchase will be. Customer usage and product disposal costs will also be assessed at this time. Forecasts of future revenues will be established based upon this market analysis.

The assessment of product costs and how they will change over time is not a precise science. There are three approaches that can be used: analogy, parametric modeling, and industrial engineering. Life cycle costing is a relatively new technique and companies are experi-menting with new methods of cost assessment.

The *analogy method* uses historical information from another product that has similar characteristics to the new product (or product family). The assumption is made that the cost patterns observed in the analogous product will be repeated in the new product. This approach is quick and easy to use (providing the his-torical information is readily available) and the costs are based on something "real." The downfall of the method is, of course, find-ing analogous products. It is often impossible to find a single prod-uct that can reliably represent the pattern of the new product. Sometimes it is necessary to combine the historical data from more than one product to build up the pattern of cost over the product's life cycle. But it is difficult to be confident that the analogous pat-tern is valid.

Parametric modeling is gaining popularity for life cycle costing. These models, originally developed for economic analysis, seek to understand the parameters that drive costs and revenues and use projections of the values of these parameters to determine the life cycle costs. In a simple example of this approach, a company mak-ing baby products will carefully consider birth rate projections and family demographics when developing new products. Another example is the reliance put on forecasts of building starts by construction materials manufacturers.

Parametric modeling can provide excellent results if the parameters are well understood. Another advantage is that the projections used are often available to the public from government and academic research organizations and do not require costly research by the company. These models, however, are often very complex and subtle. Specialized skills are required to develop and maintain the model. The complexity increases dramatically as the number of parameters increases because the interrelationship between the parameters must be understood. Powerful computers and sophisticated programs are required to develop the model and to perform the sensitivity analysis that is needed to validate the model and to assess its accuracy.

The third approach is the traditional *industrial engineering cost "rollup."* Once the product is designed in detail it is possible for the detailed costs to be calculated from the product's bill of materials and production process. Other costs, like transportation costs and disposal costs, can be calculated from the physical characteristics of the product. Future changes in such issues as labor costs, fuel costs, material costs, etc. can be made so that the total product costs can be projected over the life cycle of the product.

This method cannot be done until after the product is fully designed. It requires a considerable amount of time and effort to roll up all the costs associated with the product and create the final life cycle model. This approach is, however, well understood and has obvious validity to the people using the numbers.

Whichever method (or combination of methods) is used, it is important to realize that these projections are far from accurate. They do, however, provide a better basis for decision making than no information at all. Companies using life cycle costing for strategic purposes find that it is important to constantly revise the projections as real data becomes available. In the early stages of product launch the incoming data will not be very helpful, but once reliable information is established the life cycle cost model can be continuously updated and refined.

Owing to the nature of a life cycle cost model it is vital that the model be developed by a cross-functional team and not by the accountants alone. This is an example of the power of a concurrent engineering team composed of people from many different disciplines within the company.

Figure 8-7. Life Cycle Costing Requires a Cross-Functional Team

Quality Function Deployment

Quality function deployment (QFD) is a formalized method of matching the expressed needs of the customer to the features and functions of the product. Classic QFD uses a diagram called the "house of quality" (see Figure 8-8), which lists the customer's expectations of the product down the left-hand side of the chart. The planned product features are shown on the chart and matched to customer needs. Other aspects like competitive analysis, functional interaction, and priorities are also shown on the chart. This sophisticated visual method keeps the team's eyes squarely focused on the customer needs.

> ## Quality Function Deployment (QFD)
>
> A formal approach to hearing the voice of the customer throughout the design and product development process

These are the steps required for a QFD project:

- *Assess customer needs.*
  This can be done through a market research survey, by interviews with current customers, or by less direct methods. It is vital to have good customer needs information. When drawing the chart it is helpful to use the customer's exact words as much as possible.

- *Categorize customer needs.*
  For purposes of clarity the customer's expressed needs are organized into different categories by the team. The use of an affinity diagram is often helpful for this task (Mizuni 1979).

- *Prioritize customer needs.*
  Each item on the list is prioritized according to importance. It may be necessary to go back to the customer for input at this stage. A simple prioritizing method with scores from 1 to 5 is best.

- *Perform current competitive analysis.*
  This is a "reality check" to see how your current products compare to competitive products based upon customer needs.

- *Establish relationships.*
  As the design project progresses it is important to show how the features of the design relate to the customer's expressed needs. The features of the newly designed product are entered onto the chart and matches established to show how these features meet the customer's needs.

- *Assess importance of design requirements.*
  The importance of each design requirement can be assessed from the importance the customers place on a feature and the degree to which each feature provides competitive edge.

- *Correlate design requirements.*
  The roof of the house chart is used to show the correlation between design features: which augment each other and which are contrary to each other.

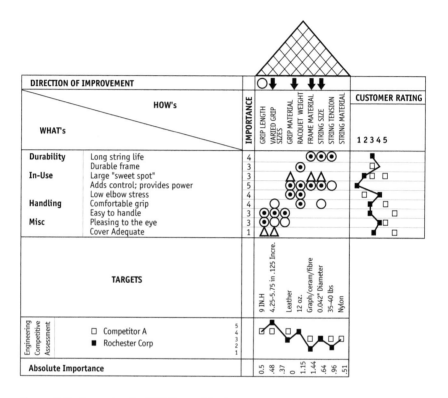

Figure 8-8. Example of a QFD House Chart

From this systematic analysis the final chart can be drawn. QFD charts are usually drawn by hand, and they are often drawn and redrawn throughout the development process. The purpose of the exercise is not to create pretty pictures but to involve the team in a study of how the product matches the customer's needs.

The accountants on the team often prove adept at the use of house charts. Despite the technical nature of the features being discussed, the accountants and other professionals can provide analysis and support to the engineers in matching the needs of the customers to the features of the product.

Variety Effectiveness Analysis

As the number of products a company manufactures increases there is a considerable challenge just coping with all the different parts, processes, and products. Henry Ford was able to be amazingly productive by having a single product (any color you want providing its black) and perfecting the production process for that single product. Today's manufacturers must be as effective as Ford (or better) with a wide variety of products.

There is a positive aspect to variety and a negative aspect. Positive variety is the ability to offer the customers a wider range of custom or focused products. Negative variety is the complexity and confusion caused by having many different products, processes, components, and distribution channels. We need to be able to provide positive variety to our customers while limiting the negative variety effects upon the production and distribution processes.

An example of negative variety is taken from a Canadian company that manufactures drilling bits for oil rigs and other deep drilling facilities. This company used to have fifteen product families of drilling bits, each containing several different kinds of bits. These families each had different engineering characteristics. A product-rationalization program revealed that the customers were bewildered by the variety of bits available and were uncertain when to use each kind. The company redesigned its products, reducing the product line to only three product families. Each of these families was then reengineered to fill a broad range of tasks. The customers were happy because they only had to stock three different kinds of drilling bits instead of fifteen. In turn, the company gained substantial savings by making, stocking, and marketing far fewer products.

Electronics companies often find significant duplication of parts and components: the same item with more than one part number, and interchangeable components that are shown separately. One company had 1500 different item numbers for resistors and 120 of these were 1,000Ω resistors. Through a detailed variety effectiveness program the company reduced their resistor item list from 1500 to 200. The savings associated with this reduction were enormous. Many of the savings were intangible and difficult to quantify and included such things as reducing complexity and confusion within inventory control, purchasing, and production. Others were clear savings in inventory holding costs, better purchasing costs, fewer people needed to control the part numbers, and so forth. Some products had increased materials costs as a result of these changes but these additional costs were far outweighed by the broader savings accrued from the increase in commonality and reduction of variety within the process.

The same principles apply within the production processes. If the number of different processes can be reduced and more commonality of process introduced within the organization's product range, then the company will see enormous reductions in tangible and intangible costs. In addition, increased process commonality makes the company more flexible as customer product-mix and product-volume needs change.

Role of the Accountant in Variety Effectiveness

The analysis required to assess the companies variety effectiveness —both the positive and negative varieties—is a subtle and complex task. There is a need to review the parts, products, and processes to determine commonality, position of variability in the production process, variety benefits from the customer's perspective, and the financial impact of current variety. These analyses require the kind of analytic skills accountants have developed throughout their training.

Working with a team of engineers and production people, the accountants can bring a valuable perspective to the analysis. In particular the accountants can develop methods for understanding the relative costs and benefits of different approaches. Very often it is difficult to understand the cost impact of the current confusion and the benefits of undertaking the enormous task of eliminating unneeded variety. The accountants can assess the impact of the tangible and intangible costs. In addition, the analysis of the products, parts, and processes does not require engineering skills; it requires skills in the kind of statistical analysis that accountants use daily.

Continuous Improvement

The objective of concurrent engineering and cross-functional teams is to design the product "right the first time" so that it is perfect when first put into production: perfect quality, perfect production process, perfect features, and perfect cost.

We do not, however, live in a perfect world. While concurrent engineering has radically improved product design and reduced time-to-market it is not uncommon for products to go into production without achieving their allowed cost. The process of target costing and value engineering eliminates much of the excess cost but often there is more improvement that can be made.

Once the design project is complete the processes of continuous improvement come into action. Target costs can continue to be set after the product is in production. Target costing systems can have effectivity dates established so that cost improvements can continue to be worked on throughout the production processes. Value engineering teams can continue to extract costs from the product and the process. Even after the allowed cost is achieved more improvement can be created.

Continuous improvement is a basic tenet of the *total quality management* movement. Everybody in the company is responsible for improving quality and eliminating waste. Waste costs money. Eliminating waste reduces costs. The accountants need to be on quality improvement teams studying the products, production processes, and administrative processes; continuously eliminating waste and improving quality. This is how accountants can become valuable, proactive professionals creating improvement and moving the company forward.

Summary

The proliferation of new products and the need for fast time-to-market has led companies to adopt concurrent engineering methods of product design. Concurrent engineering requires a cross-functional team of professionals to work on product design from start to finish. Accountants have an important role to play on the concurrent engineering teams.

As well as being team members involved in every aspect of product design, accountants perform specific tasks requiring the use of new accounting techniques developed specifically for concurrent engineering methods. These include:

- Target costing
- Value engineering
- Life cycle costing
- Quality function deployment
- Variety effectiveness analysis

These new approaches provide vital insight into the quest for products that are enthusiastically accepted by the market, have very high levels of quality, can be made and distributed profitably, and reach the market quickly. In addition, the analytical skills of accountants can be used in many other aspects of the design process. This opens up exciting new avenues where accounting professionals can make a vital contribution to the company's success.

Questions

1. Why are progressive companies using new approaches to product design?

2. What is concurrent engineering? List some keys to success with concurrent engineering.

3. Define target profit, allowable cost, and target cost. How could target costing principles be best applied in your company?

4. List three benefits of life cycle costing. Is life cycle costing applicable in your company? How would you begin to model life cycle costs of new products; by analogy, heuristically, by calculation, or another approach?

5. How can house charts be used in your company to understand and focus on customer needs?

6. Does the accounting department have customers? How can the accounting department become more customer focused? Would a house chart be helpful in matching your department's "product" to the needs of the customer?

9

Implementing the New Approach to Accounting

There are two ways that these new approaches to the role of the accountant in a world class company can be achieved; strategically or pragmatically. If these changes are introduced strategically then they are driven from the top of the company. Senior managers catch a vision for a world class organization and see that the role of accountants—and others—needs to change dramatically if the company is to succeed in its quest for world class status. The changes are coordinated and companywide. A new role is defined for the accounting people (or *by* the accounting people) and these changes are introduced with education and training, the initiation of improvement projects, and the reorganization of the accounting department and the integration of previously accounting functions into the operations departments. The strategic approach is fast, radical, and culture changing.

The description of this process given in the previous paragraph sounds very simple, straightforward, and problem-free. Nothing

189

could be further from the truth. During the Gulf War we were introduced to the idea of a "surgical strike," conjuring up the idea of a clean and tidy war in which only a few people get hurt; no civilians, only people with black hats. In reality a surgical strike is the deployment of monstrously powerful and hugely destructive weapons that create appalling mayhem and carnage. The same is true of the strategic approach to radical change in the accounting department (or other support areas) of a company. The process is painful, unnerving, fraught with risk and difficulty, and generally occurs when the company is in a critical state. However, strategic and coordinated change is more likely to succeed than ill-focused opportunistic change.

The people involved in radical change need to be committed to making the changes work. They must have a clear understanding of the strategic objectives, and they must be prepared to change their role, their status, and their activities. For most people these are difficult changes, but they can be made less problematic if they are part of a clear strategy of change, improvement, and restructuring leading to a healthier and more agile organization, ready to meet the challenges of the future.

When the strategic approach to change is made, there can be enormous success and improvement throughout the organization. The reengineering experienced by many companies in the 1990s has been a mixed blessing. Some companies have emerged greatly improved; others have merely "downsized" and are no more vibrant than before. They may have averted short-term disaster but they have not gained the fundamental revitalization promised by the reengineering exercise. Often companies do not have the vision and organizational competency to make the kinds of changes required to radically improve their business. But very significant improvement can still be made within the organization by managers who see the opportunity and understand the need to make creative change. It is not necessary to have fundamental and strategic change taking place in the company for the accounting people to reengineer their own roles, for instance, and become more valuable members. They can gradually introduce changes within the organization, change their own role and position within the company, and recreate themselves from being backward-looking number crunchers into forward-looking, proactive, valuable members of the organization.

Making the Change

Regardless of the origin of the changes taking place in the accounting community, the activities described below are the starting point for creating a new proactive role for accountants. There is no particular sequence to these activities and it is not necessary for all the initiatives to be employed. Every company is different and the specific approaches will be governed by the needs of the company and its market. The rest of this chapter is taken up with practical suggestions of actions any accountant can take to change their role and reengineer their own job and position in the company.

Getting Ready

The following activities are things that accountants can do to prepare themselves for making the changes described in this book. These changes are not easy to make, but they can be made easier if the people involved have actively chosen to change their ideas and their outlook.

Read Widely

It is common for most professional people within an organization to read magazines and books about the issues associated with their profession. Accountants read such magazines as *Management Accounting* or *Accounting Today* and they read books dealing with new ideas on accounting topics. But this is not sufficient. If real change is to occur it is necessary to begin to read and understand the issues associated with a wider range of disciplines.

It is well known that real change and improvement never comes from the center of a discipline. Real changes—the paradigm shifts —are made by people on the periphery. Creative ideas rarely come from people who are the experts in a particular field; they often cannot see the forest for the trees. Creative change comes from people who are able to synthesize ideas from one aspect of business (or life in general) with ideas from another area. These ideas may not seem to naturally fit together; sometimes they actually appear to be in conflict. But this is the crucible of creativity in any walk of life.

Another similar approach is to attend trade associations aimed at other professionals, perhaps with people from your company who are working in very different fields from accounting. Take classes in nonaccounting subjects. Most larger companies have a well planned education and training program for their employees; take classes designed for production people, engineers, sales people, and so forth. If these classes are not available directly through your company, then seek them out at local colleges, universities, and adult education centers.

Deliberately read books that will broaden your scope of knowledge, particularly books that relate to nonaccounting aspects of your business. Make sure you understand the technology associated with the products your company makes. Make time to understand the production methods and philosophies employed in the company. Read books that are quite outside the realm of your company; books that will stimulate new ideas and new approaches.

Cultivate a Global View

Recognize that the world has changed radically and every company is in a global market. Gain an understanding of the global issues affecting your company and your marketplace. Seek out information that will broaden your own understanding of the challenges your company is facing in the global market place. *The Economist* newspaper is a good place to start.

Spend as much time as possible with the sales and marketing people of the company, not discussing variances or profitability, but discussing the issues they are facing day in and day out in the market. Delve deeply into the issues of competitiveness of the products, the value your company provides to the customer, the gaps in the market, new products in the making, and the changes in technology that are likely to affect the company's market position and competitiveness.

Study the company's competitors. Become an expert in the competition's plans, strategies, and financial position. Get the information needed to understand what your competitors are doing and how their approaches differ from those of your own company.

Spend time with the design engineers and other people in the R&D departments. Gain an understanding of the issues that are challenging your company. Investigate the historical development of the company's products, their attributes, why they were successful or failures, and what is being done to overcome limitations in the market. Examine the new technologies and ideas being developed by the R&D people, and understand how these new products will affect the marketplace.

Go to the shop floor and the warehouses more often. Understand the processes, understand the people's view and approach, and become familiar with the issues they are facing. Perhaps volunteer to work a few shifts, perhaps the evening shift, so that you can become more intimately familiar with the shopfloor processes and procedures.

Create a Team

If you are finding a need within your company to take a radically different role, then it is likely that there are other people with similar feelings. Make a point of discussing these issues in a nonthreatening way with the people in your department and other related departments. If there is interest in pursuing these kinds of changes then create a small team of enthusiastic volunteers. Work together to make these changes. Some people start a small study group that meets once a week to discuss the issues. These study groups often include a reading circle where (outside of the group meeting) the people read a practical book on TQM, or cellular manufacturing, or activity-based management, or another important topic, and then come together to discuss the book and its relevance to their own situation.

It is easier to introduce these kinds of changes when you have a group of people working together than it is if an individual is working alone. Creating a group of like-minded company employees is a valuable step to creating change. Make sure the group remains positive. It is easy for a group of this sort to become focused on the company's shortcomings; every company has plenty of room for improvement. The best companies are the most self-critical. It is important the group focuses on the need for change and the opportunities for change.

Learn the Techniques of Modern Manufacturing Management

Read the books and take the classes so that you become very familiar with the current trends in modern manufacturing. The accounting (and other) support people in a company are often criticized for being ignorant of the methods and ideas the company is pursuing. This must be overcome. A starting point would be total quality management methods. If there are no classes available, use one of the many excellent books on TQM to gain an in-depth understanding of its processes and procedures (see Bibliography for some suggested titles). Apply these methods in your own workplace first so that you have first-hand practical knowledge of the subject.

Learn about statistical process control (SPC). SPC is the foundation for the development of quality processes in industrial organizations. Most companies use SPC in production areas only; but SPC is quite applicable to a wide range of business situations (see Wheeler 1993). It is important that proactive accountants have a good understanding of the methods, strengths, and limitations of SPC.

Learn and use the Seven Management Tools (see Brassard 1989; Mizuno 1979). These are methods that have been developed to apply the philosophies of TQM in the broader context of management creativity and process improvement. While classic TQM is concerned with gathering numerical data, analyzing it, and creating improvement from an understanding of statistics, the Seven Management Tools are concerned with gathering and analyzing qualitative information about the business and using this for creating improvement and radical change. These innovative methods of problem solving and team-based improvement are powerful tools for any agent of change.

Learn the concepts involved with production planning and control. If your company is currently endeavoring to use an MRPII approach, then read the books about traditional MRPII methods (see Arnold 1991; Vollmann 1992). If the company is moving towards world class or agile manufacturing methods then study those issues and understand the concepts and the practicalities (see Maskell 1994; Schonberger 1986). Many of these important new approaches are delayed or compromised because the accounting people do not have a clear understanding of the real goals of the changes, and concentrate only on the accounting issues.

Process Map Your Own Department's Activities

The best place to start putting these new methods into action is within your own department. Don't just read the books and enjoy them; actively use the methods and gain a practical understanding of the techniques. The first reason for process mapping your own department is to gain an understanding of how to use process mapping for process improvement. Try not to do this alone. These process mapping methods and the TQM ideas are designed for team-based improvement and work best when used by a small team. Try to create enthusiasm within your department for working together to understand the fundamental issues within your own areas and create improvement.

Once the process maps have been drawn, use the analytical tools to gain an understanding of flow of work through the department. Determine value-added and non-value-added processes, assign primary and secondary classifications, and draw graphs of these measures. Look at the timeliness of the activities your department performs, understand the delays, understand the quality problems and where they occur. Drill down deeply in the issues your department is facing. If necessary, bring in some people from outside the area to provide a fresh look at the issues. Ask "why" five times and get to root causes of problems; even if the answers are uncomfortable.

Once the analysis has been done it is usually quite straightforward to develop new processes and procedures that will overcome many of the problems including non-value-added, quality problems, delays, and so forth. If there is no appetite for radical change within the department, it may not be possible to implement these changes fully, but that should not prevent the people in the department from developing the ideas and presenting them to the managers with the back-up analysis. Or employ the Jesuit school of management approach: Since forgiveness is easier to obtain than permission, do it first and ask permission later.

Visit Other Companies

There are probably many excellent companies close to where you work. Make a habit of visiting customers and vendors. Initially these visits may have to be arranged through the sales people or the purchasing people. They may want to be with you when you visit. But after a time as these ideas become more widespread it will be possible for you to visit the customers or the vendors and provide them with positive help or assistance, and you will learn from them at the same time.

When you read about companies in trade journals and other magazines, call the people mentioned in the magazine and discuss the issues that are raised in the article. If possible, arrange to make a visit. It does not have to be a long visit, one or two hours is sufficient. Most people are very willing to show off the good things they have achieved.

Speak to people at your trade association meetings. Find out about their companies. Visit the ones that are doing innovative and interesting things. Listen to what your opposite numbers at these companies are complaining about; these might be just the issues you need to look at and understand.

What's an Accountant to Do?

The following suggestions are not in any particular order and it is not intended that they should all be applied. You need to tailor the approach to your own company's needs. But these are tried and tested methods of making improvements and creating relevance for the accounting people within the company.

Simplify Systems

Start making improvements in your own backyard. Take a long, hard, analytical look at your own processes and procedures. Draw the process maps, simplify the processes and eliminate the waste. There is no magic involved here. It is the systematic application of common sense and a willingness to take a new look at old paradigms.

Use the content of Chapter 4 to establish a way to simplify accounting procedures. If the company is pursuing these changes strategically and systematically, then establish a plan to radically simplify the accounting processes. If the company has a smaller vision, then begin to simplify your own areas and work with the operations people to make your processes focused, understandable, and simple.

Use Statistical Process Control (SPC) for Tracking

The use of statistical process control (SPC) outside of production operations is quite rare. Yet the methods of SPC apply widely throughout any company. SPC is dealing with understanding the variability of a process—any process—and monitoring the stability of that process. This applies to clerical and administrative processes just as much as production processes. In his book *Understanding Variation*, Don Wheeler shows the importance of understanding any numerical information in the context of the variability and stability of that information. This includes such information as financial reports, inventory levels, inventory accuracy, and other performance measures.

Study the reports your department produces for your own use and the use of your "customers" throughout the company and assess the applicability of SPC to the presentation of this information. Analyze the data over the last year or so, draw control charts, and gain an understanding of the variability of the data. It is useful to ask the question "What would the company have done differently over the last year if we had presented the information using SPC?" The answer to this question will be a guide to the applicability of SPC to your own environment.

Standardize Reporting

Many people find the reports presented to them by the accounting department confusing and complicated. Try to simplify them. Once simplification has been completed, address standardization. If all the reports and information throughout the company were presented in a standard and clear way there would be much less confusion about the information being presented.

This is particularly true of the performance measures used throughout the company. If your department is responsible for the production of some (or all) of the performance measurement reports then take a look at how they can be standardized. Standard presentation is always useful even if the information is quite different: presenting that information in a standard format can provide clarity and understanding. For example, four graphics on a single page for each department showing quality, cost, timeliness, and customer satisfaction measures can be used throughout the organization even though the calculation of those measures may vary considerably from one department to another.

Standardizing the assumptions behind the reported information can be very helpful. Too much valuable time is wasted when the same information is reported in two different ways. Reporting revenues with or without customer returns is a simple example of this kind of confusion. The company then has meetings to discuss the differences, often with some acrimony amongst the various parties involved. One way to simplify is to standardize the approach and standardize the data so that everyone is using the same information presented in the same way.

Eliminate Reports

Most company produce too many reports. The reports are often confusing and conflicting. Create a project to review the company's performance measurement methods. If it is possible, set up a team to do a full performance measurement development program as described in Chapter 7. If it is not possible to create so elaborate a project, do at least develop the linkages between the company's strategic directions and the critical success factors (CSF); and then assess the performance measurement approach in light of the strategically-based CSFs.

Review the company's current measurement system against these critical issues, taking account of the seven criteria presented in Chapter 7. From this analysis you will be able to significantly reduce the number and complexity of the reports used throughout the company, and will be able to focus on reporting relevant and strategically important issues.

Measure Your Department's Performance

While many accounting and finance departments are very much involved in the performance measurement of the company they often do not have methods of measuring their own performance. Remember that the accounting department provides a service to its "customers" inside and outside of the company. As a service department, it needs to understand its customers and their needs, and have methods of assessing how well these needs are being met.

The basic measurements of quality, on-time delivery, cost, and customer service can be applied to the accounting department quite straightforwardly. Take the regular and repetitive aspects of the department's business and make quantitative measures of timeliness, errors, and effectiveness.

For a service department it is usually most effective to measure quality in terms of customer satisfaction. This can be measured by constructing a simple survey of the people in the company (and outside the company) that use the accounting department. These will be managers looking for information, people submitting expense reports, vendors looking for payment, and so forth. The survey needs to be short and easy so that it addresses the issues but is not burdensome to the customers. Address issues like timeliness, completeness, relevance, and people issues like user friendliness, understanding of the business, willingness to help people outside your own responsibilities and "go the second mile."

Standardize Department Processes

A key to quality and understanding within an organization is standardization of the business processes. Within the accounting department the standardization of processes is equally important. It is often thought that the accounting area of a company is the most standardized because the work is governed by accounting standards like FASB and SSAP, and so forth. This is only partly true. While these standards do regulate the outcome of the department's work, they do not regulate the way the work is done, nor should they.

Study your own department and delve more deeply into how the department functions. Study the written procedures and compare them with the actual methods used. From this study develop new procedures that can standardize the way work is done across the department. This will require the writing of new procedures and the development of training materials so that people can be trained to work in the new, standardized way. This is not a single task. Devise a mechanism for constantly standardizing and improving the methods. Once these standardized approaches have been introduced and seen to succeed then the same methods can be applied to other departments and other processes.

Study Month-End Close

The month-end close in many companies is an elaborate and puzzling ritual of closings, reconciliations, and post-closing entries. The ultimate goal is to have a financial reporting system that does not require a "close" as such because it is constantly up-to-date and does not require batch or manual journal entries at month-end.

The month-end closing is often fraught with tension because the senior managers are anxious to get the month-end (or worse yet, quarter-end) information and they want it quickly. While the objective is to eliminate the month-end process by providing everybody in the company with accurate up-to-date information all the time, it can be valuable to significantly reduce the month-end process activities as a beginning.

Start by setting a goal to halve the time required to do the month-end close. Typically this requires halving the elapse time for month-end; but halving the working time would also be a good goal. Study the process, analyze the activities, and map the flow of information, time, effort, and quality. Working as a team, devise methods to eliminate the time taken to achieve the month-end reports. It is important to actually eliminate activities and waste, not merely make the process quicker.

Understand Company Processes and Core Competencies

The charge that the accountants are divorced from reality and do not know anything about the company's real business must be resolved. Make a point of learning how your own company works. There is only a certain amount that can be learned from books; the real issues are learned from working with the people in the company, understanding their issues and problems, and resolving those problems. Make a habit of getting out of your own area of the company and out to where the people really work. Ask them to spend time explaining their work to you. This can either be done straightforwardly by making time to go out and ask them directly, or it can be done when there is another company issue involved. For example, if there are significant cost variances for a product line or production area, instead of waiting for the variance meetings, go to the department and work with them to understand and resolve the issue in a positive, learning way. This way you will learn about the issues the department is facing, understand their processes, and (perhaps) be helpful to them.

There are several areas that accounting people must fully understand and appreciate. Production and materials planning is one area. Work with the people doing the sales and operations planning, master scheduling, and capacity planning to fully understand how production and materials are planned. Most companies do not do sales and operations planning very effectively. It is rare for the financial people to be involved in the sales and operations process; but it is a mistake for accounting not to be involved in the process. The outcome of a monthly sales and operations planning process can be very good estimates of profitability and cash flow derived from real production plans; this is valuable information. Gain an understanding, get involved, make improvements.

Another area of expertise for accountants in manufacturing companies is the business systems. These are often called Manufacturing Resource Planning systems (MRPII) or Enterprise Resource Planning systems (ERP) and it is important to understand how your system works and how it is integrated with the financial accounting systems. In many companies, of course, the financial and cost accounting systems are a part of the ERP system, but that does not mean that the accounting people have any clear idea of the methods and philosophies behind the system. Go out and spend time with the people doing the planning, the shopfloor entry, the warehousing and receiving activities, the sales order entry and quoting; learn and understand.

The planning leads into shop floor control. How are the products controlled in the production area? Who does the detailed scheduling, how is it done, and what tools do they have at their disposal? How do the shopfloor systems link into the planning and inventory systems? What is the "real" inventory accuracy? Not the year-end physical which, in many companies, is done to satisfy the auditors, but the real accuracy in the stockroom and on the floor.

If your company is moving towards world class manufacturing methods then you need to understand these methods because they are vital to the company's success and they have profound accounting implications. Once again, reading the books is not enough. Go and work with the people who are establishing the cells, help with shopfloor layout perhaps, understand how the cells can be scheduled using production rates instead of traditional work orders, gain firsthand experience of the problems and difficulties of making these changes in practice.

Define Roles of Accounting Department

It is important to understand the mission of your work if you are to be effective. If the goals and objectives of the accounting and finance group are not well defined and understood by the people in the department and throughout the company, then there is a need to develop and disseminate this definition. It takes a considerable amount of time and clear thinking to develop a definition of the role of the accounting department (or any other department). Time and clear thinking can often be scarce commodities. But it is important to create a jointly developed and understood philosophy for everything the department does.

Link this role definition to the strategic needs of the business and to the needs of the department customers. The "customers" of the finance and accounting department are mostly within the company, but also include outside parties such as the IRS, the SEC, company suppliers, and other partners. Make sure the department's goals and objectives match the requirements of the customers and the company strategy. Once this is achieved, measure the time spent on the activities that are strategically important; this is the equivalent of "value-added" work in a department that is entirely non-value-adding.

Introduce a 5S Program into Accounting

The idea of 5S (or industrial housekeeping) is to have a clearly defined and tidy workplace. The 5S's refer to the Japanese words for five concepts—organization, orderliness, cleanliness, standardized cleanup, and discipline—that lead to a planned and organized work environment. The 5S approach has been used primarily on the shop floor where work areas are cleaned and tidied, the materials and tools are arranged conveniently, and only items required immediately are present. The thinking behind this is that people work better and more effectively if their work spaces are well organized, that safety is enhanced when an area is orderly, that work is more efficient if the tools and materials required to do the job are readily available, and that equipment is more long-lived if it is cleaned and cared for each day.

There is no reason why this approach should be any less important in an office environment than a production area. There have been many highly successful introductions of 5S in administrative offices, product design departments, marketing areas, and accounting groups. Start by educating people on the ideas of 5S. Some people are offended by the suggestion that their work area is untidy and other people do not see the significance of the approach; these people need to understand the reasons for making this change. Move through the 5S program step by step. Introduce basic tidiness first, then move to "a place for everything and everything in its place," and finally move onto the full 5S approach. Use a measurement method so that offices can be assessed on their adherence to 5S. Create a planned and orderly environment.

Cross-Train

Provide cross-training within your own area. The more broadly based an accountant can be, the more useful and valuable he or she will be to the company. The starting point for cross-training is within the accounting group itself. Develop a plan for the people in the various accounting functions to cross-train each other and create a program for moving from one set of tasks to another within the department.

Make sure that everyone in the department understands that the purpose of doing this is to provide more flexibility and expertise within the department, and to be a starting point for a more profound cross-training when the accounting people will move outside of the walls of their department. Recognize that some people will not want to participate. If this is a small number, then just allow them to stay outside of the program. If it is a large number of people, then there is more work to be done with education and persuasion to convince these people of the necessity to move into a proactive role.

Move Accountants into Operational Departments

Look at the practicality of moving the accounting functions into the operational areas of the company. It is best to move the accounting functions both physically and in terms of reporting and departments; but if this is not possible politically, then move the people physically while retaining the original reporting structure. The benefit of this is that the accounting people can then be involved in the daily business of the company making products, shipping to customers, provisioning materials, tracking schedules, and so forth.

In most companies the only problems encountered in making this move are political problems. Moving the cost and management accounting people into the area of the company they work on makes obvious sense and can be justified merely in terms of the time required to travel backwards and forwards. Moving the accounts payable people into the purchasing and receiving area can be more difficult to achieve, and moving the accounts receivable function into sales and marketing can also present some problems.

But making these moves shows a real commitment to being involved and relevant.

Volunteer to Join Improvement Teams

An excellent way for an accountant to become more and more involved with the business is to get involved with improvement teams. In companies committed to TQM and continuous improvement there are often *kaizen* teams that proliferate for improvement throughout the organization. It is easy to join these teams and make a contribution. In more traditional companies it takes more effort to become involved in improvement activities because they often do not have a cross-functional approach and do not see a need to involve people not directly associated with the problem. The only way to get into these teams is to volunteer and make a contribution; become known as the helpful accountant.

Fruitful areas for involvement are such projects as an Inventory Accuracy team that is designed to understand why inventory records become inaccurate and how to permanently solve the problem of the physical on-hand figures being at variance with the computer records.

Sales and operations planning is another project where the accountants can be very helpful. This is the establishment of a formal method for understanding the sales demand on the company, understanding the company's production capacity and capability, and matching these to the company's business strategy. The outcome of this monthly process is a medium term production plan that has been agreed to by the sales and marketing people, the production operations people, the new product development people, and the senior management of the company. Most companies do this badly; join a team that will address these issues and make the process very good.

There are, of course, hosts of other areas where an accountant can become involved, make a contribution, and learn something important about the company, its methods and procedures, and its people. Don't wait to be asked to join a team. Go out and volunteer—get involved.

Presentations on Accounting Methods for Company Personnel

If you are looking to be cross-trained and to gain understanding of the company's business and processes, the chances are that there are people from other company departments with similar aspirations. Provide methods for other people in the company to learn about the methods and techniques associated with the finance department. Be careful not to make these meetings a kind of *accounting for the nonfinancial manager* class. The purpose of the sessions is to open up the mysteries of the company accounting methods so that there can be an exchange of ideas and to gather improvement opportunities.

Consider the people attending these sessions as your "customers." Determine what they are looking for from the accounting department. Listen to their complaints and frustrations about the current accounting approaches and the people involved in them. Create improvement teams to address and solve the problems raised by the "customers."

Create Teams

Even companies that developed teamwork as a fundamental part of their business and improvement activities do not see these approaches flowing into the service and support departments of the company. There is every reason to think that a team-based approach will work very well in the accounting department.

There are two kinds of teams: improvement teams and work teams. Start with improvement teams. Set up improvement teams to address the issues facing the accounting department and to create improvement. These teams may be responsible for continuous improvement efforts that make continuous incremental changes within the organization; or they may be radical improvement teams aimed at making quantum improvements to the business. Make sure the teams are cross-functional by bringing in people from outside the financial area to help with the improvement process.

This kind of initiative can be done easily if the company is committed to team-based improvement, but is more difficult to establish if there is little emphasis on these kinds of approaches. More difficult in any environment is the use of self-directed work teams. In a self-directed work-team, a group of people work together cross-functionally with team-based objectives and without a hierarchical management structure. This kind of approach is not suitable for all companies and requires a commitment to empowerment and radical change. The benefits of self-directed teams are that they are very flexible and can accommodate large variations of workload, they are very suitable for combining several different kinds of work in one group, and they provide significant opportunities for empowering people to control and improve their own work.

Start Activity-Based Management

Activity-based management (ABM) is a powerful tool for enabling the accounting people within the company to become actively involved with the operations of the business and to help with the development of both radical and continuous improvement. Assess the feasibility of conducting an ABM pilot study. Select a process that is large enough to be significant to the company but is small enough to be effectively analyzed by a cross-functional team over a three month period.

Once the pilot has been established and is seen to be successful, it will be possible to begin the process of expanding the use of ABM throughout the organization. It is achieving the initial success that is difficult. There may need to be some training and education required to explain the ideas and purpose of ABM before people will commit time and money to the project. It may be necessary to "sell" the concept to the senior managers of the company and the people in the company who will be the recipients of the project's conclusions.

It is often helpful to have some of the people in the company visit another organization that has been successful with ABM so that the actual benefits can be seen. If need be, start ABM with a less ambitious pilot project that can be achieved quickly and easily without the large amount of commitment and expenses associated with a larger project. While a small pilot will have limited results, it can be used to demonstrate the method and to suggest likely approaches to success.

Use Standard Companywide Software

When *productivity software* was first introduced into companies a few years back people tended to select the software programs that suited their needs. As personal computers became widespread within companies, the problem developed where everybody used their own favorite programs. This created a wide range of varying protocols without any method of integrating the files and other outputs from these programs. This has been particularly true within accounting and finance departments that were early users of spreadsheets and word processors.

Productivity software is jargon for programs running on personal computers that are used by individuals to help them with their work. These include word processors, spreadsheets, databases, graphic packages, presentation programs, project planning, calendars, and scheduling programs.

Most companies have now attempted to standardize these programs and systems. They have bought companywide licenses for the software packages and require everyone in the company to use the same programs. The advantage of this is that people within the company can share the files from the programs and can jointly use additional company-specific features that have been added using macros. When people are using different programs it is possible to transfer files between these programs, but they have to be converted from one protocol to another. This takes time and effort, and often does not work well.

People who are enamored of a program that has not been selected as a standard are often reluctant to change to the standard because of the amount of effort required to convert their work over to the new program, and because they do not want to have to learn a new approach. It is common within accounting departments that the standards are not adhered to. It is important that the accounting department uses the standard software so that it is easy for their "customers"—other people in the company—to use the information they produce.

Link into the Network

One of the most powerful aspects of modern computing is the local area network that links together many personal computers on people's desks. This can only be of real benefit if the primary files and information people use are on the network as shared data. If the data is kept on the local computers and not made available to others then it is less valuable.

The accounting people should make sure that all of their data and files are available to the users on the network. There is no need for secrecy (except with certain personal or sensitive data) and many benefits from having the information widely and readily available. It may be necessary for training classes to be established to show people how to access and use the information from the accounting systems and there is, of course, need for security to ensure that the data cannot be altered inadvertently.

The kind of data that can be stored on the network is the basic accounting files and ledgers, but also letters, reports, and performance measures that are associated with departments, customers, vendors, projects, and other aspects of the business.

Similarly the accountants must make use of data that is available from other departments on the network. Openness of information is an important step for the accountants to become proactive and agents of change.

Link Spreadsheets and Databases

Most accounting departments make considerable use of PC spreadsheets and databases. Very often these spreadsheets and databases are not linked to the company's primary business systems. Very often these spreadsheets are not even well linked themselves. The author has one client where the accountants used to produce more than 500 reports every month and each report used hand-entered spreadsheet data. Office productivity packages like MicroSoft Office, Lotus SmartSuite, and Novell Office are designed to have the spreadsheets, the databases, and the word processors integrated so that information is entered only once and then disseminated throughout the reporting documents.

This level of integration requires considerable knowledge of how the programs work and how they can be linked together, and it takes time and creativity to learn how to achieve this level of integration. But the time saving and clarity of information can be very significant.

Use Visual Systems in the Accounting Areas

Use of the concepts of visual systems would help to make the accounting department accessible to other people within the company. A visual approach within the offices is simply using signs, diagrams, and messages to show people where to get information, where to find people, and where different things are located. Displaying people's pictures, their roles within the department, their phone numbers and e-mail addresses, and so forth opens the department to people outside.

Posting information and performance measures on the walls of the department and around the company is very important so that people can see the results of their efforts. Display either company-wide performance or the performance of individual teams, projects, or departments. The presentation of information through graphics and diagrams helps to make the information understandable and useful to the people who need to use it. Designing forms and reports within the company for ease-of-use is another aspect of visual systems that is much neglected. Make a specific initiative to redesign the forms and reports to be easy to use.

Summary

There is a vital and exciting new role for accountants in companies that are moving away from the traditional organization and embracing world class and agile approaches to address the unpredictable marketplace of the twenty-first century. The accountant who sits isolated in his or her department printing out historical reports is becoming a relic of the past. Sadly many of these people find that their companies no longer need that kind of work done; when it is necessary it can be done readily by well designed computer systems. The accountant who can help his or her company to thrive is an accountant who can be an agent of change.

An agent of change embraces change as an opportunity, not a threat. An agent of change is willing to move into any area of the business and bring their analytical skills and unique perspective to bear on the solution to business problems. This requires a willingness to learn new tools and techniques, gain an understanding of a wide range of business issues, and to actively promulgate improvement.

These changes are taking place in every company. In most companies they are happening without any plan or recognition. In forward looking companies these changes are part of an overall plan to create a dynamic and agile team of empowered professionals ready to take on the best in the world and win. This is the future for the accountant in a world class company.

Appendix

Accounting and Measurement Questionnaire

The purpose of this questionnaire is to help the company assess where the current accounting and measurement methods stand in relation to the company's needs, and where the company needs to be in the foreseeable future.

There are twelve categories:

1. Organization
2. Timeliness
3. Budgeting
4. Cost accounting
5. Activity-based analysis
6. Performance measurement
7. Process improvement
8. Benchmarking
9. System complexity
10. Target costing and life cycle costing
11. Availability of information
12. Role of the accountants

Each category has three brief descriptions. The first description is of a company that has poor accounting and measurement methods, the second is of a company that has average methods, and the third description is of a company with a progressive approach to accounting and measurement. It is not intended that these descriptions will be 100 percent applicable to every company. They are intended as a guide to help you think out your accounting and measurement approaches in a logical, business-focused way.

Instructions

1. Read all three statements carefully—the left-hand statement defines 1 on the scale, the central statement covers the 2-4 range on the scale, and the right-hand statement defines 5 on the scale. Note: The statements and the numerical ratings do not precisely align. Some judgment is needed.
2. Honestly evaluate the present position of your organization in terms of the three statements by marking with an **X** (one of 1, 1 1/2, 2, 2 1/2, 3, 3 1/2, 4, 4 1/2 or 5) the number which best represents your *present* position.
3. Decide where you would like your organization to be *in the foreseeable future* by marking an **O** on the scale (one of 1, 1 1/2, 2, 2 1/2, 3, 3 1/2, 4, 4 1/2 or 5). This goal should be challenging, yet realistic. To illustrate this and the previous point, the following diagram shows a typical and valid response.

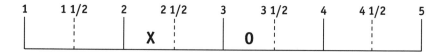

| 1 | 1 1/2 | 2 | 2 1/2 | 3 | 3 1/2 | 4 | 4 1/2 | 5 |

Accounting and Measurement

Category	Traditional			Intermediate			World Class		
Organization	The accounting department is centralized so that we have central control of the organization. The finance organization is the primary control department of the company and has fiduciary responsibility within the company.			We have a central financial accounting team responsible for financial reporting and cash analysis. Cost and management accounting is under the control of the operational managers and is located in the operational areas. We have significantly reduced the size of the accounting department because the payables and receivables functions have been moved into purchasing and customer service respectively.			We have automated the bookkeeping tasks so that the accountants spend the majority of their time on analysis and improvement projects. The people who used to be cost and management accountants now focus on operational improvement rather than reporting cost information. We have eliminated most of the payables and receivables functions by creating partnerships with our suppliers and customers to remove wasteful activities like invoicing.		
	1	1 1/2	2	2 1/2	3	3 1/2	4	4 1/2	5
Timeliness	Developing the full package of month-end reports is complex and cumbersome and we often do not have the reports complete until 2 or 3 weeks into the next month.			We have really sharpened up our month-end reporting. The reports are available within one week of the month-end close.			There is no month-end close as such because all financial reporting is available at any time to anyone. The financial postings, including any month-end adjustments, are largely automatic and month-end figures are available on the first day of the next month.		
	1	1 1/2	2	2 1/2	3	3 1/2	4	4 1/2	5

Accounting and Measurement

Category	Traditional	Intermediate	World Class
Budgeting	We have extensive and detailed budgeting for every department and cost center, and for every cost account and subaccount. This way we can plan and control our expenditure. We have a formal budget development approach so that all department managers develop their own budgets that are submitted to senior management for approval. Budget vs. actual reports are printed monthly and are reviewed in budget meetings with the responsible managers.	We have eliminated all the detailed budgeting process. There is no central control of budgets because the department managers create and control their own budgets within company guidelines. Often these local budgets are created by activity-based budgeting analysis.	We only create high level budgets for planning purposes. The company is controlled through nonfinancial measures and activity-based improvement projects. Occasionally a process improvement project will require a detailed budget for temporarily monitoring the improvement before the changes become standardized.
	1 · 1 1/2 · 2	2 1/2 · 3 · 3 1/2	4 · 4 1/2 · 5
Cost accounting	We have a thorough cost and management accounting system that requires the tracking and allocation of all costs throughout the organization. The production costs are tracked using a job costing system to monitor labor, materials, outside process, and other costs. We make extensive use of variance reports to monitor the actual costs against the standard costs and keep the manufacturing managers on their toes at the monthly variance review meetings.	We have simplified our cost and management accounting system so that we do not keep track of all the costs in detail. Most of the reporting of job costs is done automatically by the shop-floor control system. Labor costs and overheads are applied on a prorata basis from the department payroll totals. We recognize that variance analysis is unhelpful for process improvement so we have eliminated the divisive variance review meetings. Standard costs are automatically calculated by the computer system from the bills of materials and routings.	We have eliminated cost accounting completely. The computer system automatically handles the posting of direct standard product costs so that the balance sheet and P&L are kept up-to-date. We understand that if we continue to vigorously improve our operational processes then cost improvement will follow automatically without wasteful tracking and review.
	1 · 1 1/2 · 2	2 1/2 · 3 · 3 1/2	4 · 4 1/2 · 5

Accounting and Measurement

Category	Traditional			Intermediate			World Class		
Activity-based analysis	Activity-based costing (ABC) is a new way of allocating overheads to products. We don't need to do this because our standard costs already have overheads applied to them using production labor hours.			Activity-based costing (ABC) is used in our company to give us a better understanding of product costs and profitability. We have not replaced our standard costing system but have added ABC as an analysis tool.			Activity-based management (ABM) is a key driver of improvement within our company. We fully understand our major business processes and the activities that comprise them. ABM studies are conducted regularly and have created successful initiatives for both continuous improvement within departments and strategic reengineering of processes. ABC is a natural outflow of ABM and we use this information for product and customer profitability analysis.		
	1	1 1/2	2	2 1/2	3	3 1/2	4	4 1/2	5
Performance measurement	The company's primary performance measurement is done by the accounting department. We make extensive use of variance analysis, financial ratios, and other financially-based measures. We are very concerned about productivity and use measures like direct labor productivity and equipment utilization. Our primary performance measures are available monthly as a part of the month-end reports.			In addition to the financial performance measures we have a series of non-financial measures that are used at both department level and senior management level. The nonfinancial measures carry as much or more weight than the financial measures. Financial and nonfinancial measures are available when they are needed; we do not have to wait until month-end.			We run our business on primarily non-financial measures. Our performance measures have been carefully developed from the company's strategic objectives and have been consistently applied throughout the organization. We believe that if we measure the strategically important issues the company's people will work to achieve these goals, and the financial results will follow.		
	1	1 1/2	2	2 1/2	3	3 1/2	4	4 1/2	5

Accounting and Measurement

Category	Traditional			Intermediate			World Class		
Process improvement	The role of the accountant is to analyze financial information; accountants do not get involved in operational projects other than to provide financial information.			Our accounting people participate in process improvement teams. They provide financial analysis, develop benchmarking information and use activity-based analysis to contribute to the team's success.			Our accountants focus primarily on process improvement and re-engineering. They work in all aspects of operational improvement team activities. Many of the improvement projects derive from activity-based management studies that are conducted by cross-functional teams throughout the organization.		
	1	1 1/2	2	2 1/2	3	3 1/2	4	4 1/2	5
Benchmarking	We occasionally visit companies in our industry to see what they do. We often pick up a few ideas that we can put into practice. Usually they are not much better than we are, and we could teach them a thing or two.			We develop benchmarking factors from other similar companies. We recognize that there is much to be learned from companies outside of our industry because they often have similar processes to ours despite differences in product and market. This benchmark information is disseminated to the managers in the area.			Benchmarking world class companies is another key element of our operational improvement efforts. The benchmarking is done against a company with proven excellence in the area of concern. The benchmarking is carefully planned, formal, focused on specific issues, and is integrated with a process improvement team project.		
	1	1 1/2	2	2 1/2	3	3 1/2	4	4 1/2	5

Accounting and Measurement

Category	Traditional				Intermediate				World Class	
System complexity	Our business is complex and subtle; we need complex and detailed accounting and control systems to support our operation. We are a cost conscious organization and believe that every aspect of our business must be tracked and monitored to ensure efficiency and prudence.				We have simplified our accounting and control systems by addressing many of the problems at their source. We have found that if we understand the root cause of a problem we can solve it permanently. This method prevents the "disease" instead of monitoring the "symptoms."				Simplification is a cornerstone of world class effectiveness. We have worked hard to eliminate most of our accounting systems. Close partnerships with our customers, suppliers, and other third parties have enabled us to remove much of the traditional administrative waste. The computer systems have automated all of the routine accounting tasks.	
	1	1 1/2	2		2 1/2	3	3 1/2		4	4 1/2	5
Target costing and life cycle costing	We are a pragmatic company and are too busy making money to latch onto these academic new ideas.				We have begun to use target costing methods when we design products. We have an accountant on every major product design team and target costing is one of their tasks.				Now that the life cycle of our products is getting shorter and shorter we see a need to analyze and study the life cycles of products and product families. This approach is inherent within our concurrent engineering product design and development methods. Target costing is used both in a new product design and throughout a product's life cycle.	
	1	1 1/2	2		2 1/2	3	3 1/2		4	4 1/2	5

Accounting and Measurement

Category	Traditional				Intermediate			World Class		
Availability of information	The company's financial information is closely guarded. We do not allow anyone outside of senior management to see the figures in case the information is leaked to our competitors or is used against us by the unions or other parties.				We share the company's results with our employees. We create a monthly report that is presented to middle managers and supervisors by the senior staff.			We are very open with our information. Everyone in the company has access to the company's financial and performance measurement information, and we actively disseminate this information throughout the organization. We present activity-based P&L information by department, by process, and by customer. We also share this and any other information with our customers, suppliers, virtual partners, and other relevant third parties.		
	1	1 1/2	2		2 1/2	3	3 1/2	4	4 1/2	5
Role of the accountants	The accounting department is separate from the operational areas of the company. We monitor and track the operation and report to senior management through our cost and management accounting methods, and to the outside world through our financial accounts.				The accountants no longer spend the majority of their time recording and tracking data. We have simplified our cost accounting by eliminating much of the work associated with cost and variance reporting and analysis. The financial accounting has been largely automated. The accountants now spend a considerable amount of time analyzing costs and working with the operations people to help with improvement initiatives.			Most of the accountants have now all moved into operational areas where we spend most of our time on improvement projects. These improvement projects span the company from operational improvement, to target costs, to concurrent engineering, to marketing analysis.		
	1	1 1/2	2		2 1/2	3	3 1/2	4	4 1/2	5

Accounting and Measurement Diagnostics

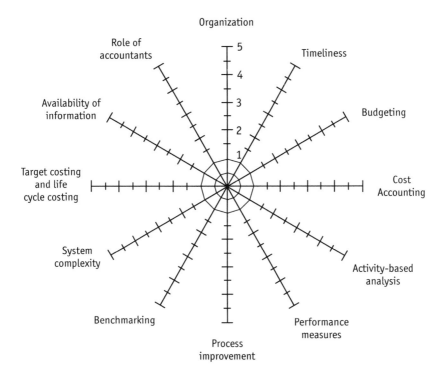

Once you have rated your company in these twelve categories by means of the Accounting and Measurement Questionnaire, mark your scores on this radar chart. If you shade in each section from the center of the chart out to your score, you will have a visual map of what your company has achieved and what it needs to do to keep improving.

Accounting and Measurement Questionnaire, copyright © 1995 by Brian Maskell Associates Inc.

References

Arnold, J. R. 1991. *Introduction to Materials Management.* Englewood Cliffs, NJ: Prentice Hall.

Brassard, Michael. 1989. *Memory Jogger Plus+.* Methuen, MA: GOAL/QPC.

Cooper, Robin. 1995. *When Lean Enterprises Collide.* Cambridge, MA: Harvard Business School Press.

Dixon, John V. 1992. (Russel Chair of Manufacturing Excellence). *Focusing Customer Service on Profits.* Unpublished article, Middle Tennessee State University.

Goldman, Nagel, and Preiss. 1995. *Agile Companies and Virtual Organizations.* Van Nostrand Reinhold.

Hartley, John R. 1992. *Concurrent Engineering.* Portland, OR: Productivity Press.

Hiromoto, Toshiro. (July 1988) "Another Hidden Edge—Japanese Management Accounting." In *Harvard Business Review.*

Ishikawa, Kaoru. 1982. *Guide to Quality Control.* White Plains, NY: Asian Productivity Organization.

Johnson, H. Thomas. 1992. *Relevance Regained*. New York: The Free Press.

Kaplan, Robert and Thomas Johnson. 1987. *Relevance Lost: The Rise and Fall of Management Accounting*. Cambridge, MA: Harvard Business School Press.

Maskell, Brian. 1994. *Software and the Agile Manufacturer*. Portland, OR: Productivity Press.

Mizuni, Shigeru. 1979. *Management for Quality Improvement: 7 New QC Tools*. Portland, OR: Productivity Press.

Monden, Yasuhiro. 1992. *Cost Management in the New Manufacturing Age*. Portland, OR: Productivity Press.

Peters, Tom. 1994. *The Tom Peters Seminar*. New York: Random House Inc.

Pine, Joseph. 1993. *Mass Customization*. Boston, MA: Harvard Business School Press.

Sakurai, Mishiharu. 1992. "Target Costing and How to Use It." In *Emerging Practices in Cost Management*, Barry J. Brinker, ed. Boston: Warren, Gorham & Lamont.

Schonberger, Richard. 1986. *World Class Manufacturing*. New York: The Free Press.

Vollman, Berry, and Whybark. 1992. *Manufacturing Planning and Control Systems*. New York: Business One Irwin.

Wheeler, Donald J. 1993. *Understanding Variation*. Knoxville, TN: SPC Press.

White, Richard. 1993. "Empirical Assessment of Just-in-Time in U.S. Manufacturers." In *Production and Inventory Management Journal*, 2nd Quarter. Falls Church, VA: APICS.

About the Author

Brian H. Maskell, President of Brian Maskell Associates, Inc., has over twenty years experience in the manufacturing and distribution industry. His management experience has ranged from the shop floor of an electronics company to Manager of European Inventories for the Xerox Corporation to Vice President of Product Development and Customer Service for the Unitronix Corporation. Over the past ten years Mr. Maskell's consulting practice has taken him to a variety of manufacturing and distribution companies in the United States, England, Mexico, Australia, South Africa and Europe. He has assisted these companies in the implementation of advanced manufacturing techniques including just-in-time manufacturing, world class and agile manufacturing methods, world class performance measurement and total quality management.

Mr. Maskell is the author of four books—*Just-in-Time: Implementing the New Strategy* (1989) from Hitchcock Publishing, *Performance Measurement for World Class Manufacturing* (1991), *Software and the Agile Manufacturer* (1994), and *New Performance Measures* (1994) from Productivity Press. He presents seminars and workshops on such subjects as Performance Measurement for World Class Manufacturing, Software and the Agile Manufacturer, the Accountant as an Agent for Change, Performance Measurement and Gainsharing, Activity-Based Management, and Just-in-Time Manufacturing. He has written numerous articles and regularly presents papers at national and international conferences.

Mr. Maskell has an engineering degree from the University of Sussex, England, is certified with the Chartered Institute of Management Accountants in London, and is a Fellow of the American Production and Inventory Control Society.

Mr. Maskell can be contacted at Brian Maskell Associates, Inc., telephone (609) 772-1244; fax (609) 772-0419; or E-mail address 72764,2200@Compuserve.com.

Index

Books from Productivity Press

Productivity Press publishes books that empower individuals and companies to achieve excellence in quality, productivity, and the creative involvement of all employees. Through steadfast efforts to support the vision and strategy of continuous improvement, Productivity Press delivers today's leading-edge tools and techniques gathered directly from industrial leaders around the world. Call toll-free 1-800-394-6868 for our free catalog.

Caught in the Middle
A Leadership Guide for Partnership in the Workplace
Rick Maurer

Managers today are caught between old skills and new expectations. You're expected not only to improve quality and services, but also to get staff more involved. This stimulating book provides the inspiration and know-how to achieve these goals as it brings to light the rewards of establishing a real partnership with your staff. Includes self-assessment questionnaires.

ISBN 1-56327-004-8 / 258 pages / $30.00 / Order CAUGHT-B269

Productivity Press, Dept. BK, P.O. Box 13390, Portland, OR 97213-0390
Telephone: 1-800-394-6868   Fax: 1-800-394-6286

Cost Reduction Systems
Target Costing and Kaizen Costing
Yasuhiro Monden

Yasuhiro Monden provides a solid framework for implementing two powerful cost reduction systems that have revolutionized Japanese manufacturing management: target costing and kaizen costing. Target costing is a cross-functional system used during the development and design stage for new products. Kaizen costing focuses on cost reduction activities for existing products throughout their life cycles, drawing on approaches such as value analysis. Used together, target costing and kaizen costing form a complete cost reduction system that can be applied from the product's conception to the end of its life cycle. These methods are applicable to both discrete manufacturing and process industries.

ISBN 1-56327-068-4 / 400 pages / $50.00 / Order CRS-B269

Delivering Customer Value: It's Everyone's Job
Karl Albrecht

Customer satisfaction results from one thing: delivering value as defined by the customer. Albrecht describes the business strategy that will create this value by knowing the customer, empowering people to deliver customer value, nurturing a service culture, and aligning the company's service systems.

ISBN 1-56327-148-6 / 72 pages / $15.95 hardcover / Order MS3P4-B269

Productivity Press, Dept. BK, P.O. Box 13390, Portland, OR 97213-0390
Telephone: 1-800-394-6868   Fax: 1-800-394-6286

Feedback Toolkit
16 Tools for Better Communication in the Workplace
Rick Maurer

In companies striving to reduce hierarchy and foster trust and responsible participation, good person-to-person feedback can be as important as sophisticated computer technology in enabling effective teamwork. Feedback is an important map of your situation, a way to tell whether you are "on or off track." Used well, feedback can motivate people to their highest level of performance. Despite its significance, this level of information sharing makes most managers uncomfortable. Feedback Toolkit addresses this natural hesitation with an easy-to-grasp 6-step framework and 16 practical and creative approaches for giving and receiving feedback with individuals and groups. Maurer's reality-tested methods in Feedback Toolkit are indispensable equipment for managers and teams in every organization.

ISBN 1-56327-056-0 / 109 pages / $12.00 / Order FEED-B269

Fast Focus on TQM
A Concise Guide to Companywide Learning
Derm Barrett

Finally, here's one source for all your TQM questions. Compiled in this concise, easy-to-read handbook are definitions and detailed explanations of over 160 key terms used in TQM. Organized in a simple alphabetical glossary form, the book can be used either as a primer for anyone being introduced to TQM or as a complete reference guide. It helps to align teams, departments, or entire organizations in a common understanding and use of TQM terminology. For anyone entering or currently involved in TQM, this is one resource you must have.

ISBN 1-56327-049-8 / 186 pages / $20.00 / Order FAST-B269

Productivity Press, Dept. BK, P.O. Box 13390, Portland, OR 97213-0390
Telephone: 1-800-394-6868   Fax: 1-800-394-6286

From Management to Leadership
Lawrence M. Miller

Miller's visionary analysis shares nine axioms of effective leadership and addresses the new requirements for leaders today. This forward-looking book shows the essential roles of vision and values, enthusiasm for customers, and teamwork and problem-solving skills at all levels.

ISBN 1-56327-103-6 / 88 pages / $15.95 / Order MS4C5-B269

The Hunters and the Hunted
A Non-Linear Solution for Reengineering the Workplace
James B. Swartz

Our competitive environment changes rapidly. If you want to survive, you have to stay on top of those changes. Otherwise, you become prey to your competitors. Hunters continuously change and learn; anyone who doesn't becomes the hunted and sooner or later will be devoured. This unusual nonfiction novel provides a veritable crash course in continuous transformation. It offers lessons from real-life companies and introduces many industrial gurus as characters. *The Hunters and the Hunted* doesn't simply tell you how to change; it puts you inside the change process itself.

ISBN 1-56327-043-9 / 582 pages / $45.00 / Order HUNT-B269

Productivity Press, Dept. BK, P.O. Box 13390, Portland, OR 97213-0390
Telephone: 1-800-394-6868   Fax: 1-800-394-6286

Implementing a Lean Management System
Thomas L. Jackson with Constance E. Dyer

Does your company think and act ahead of technological change, ahead of the customer, and ahead of the competition? Thinking strategically requires a company to face these questions with a clear future image of itself. *Implementing a Lean Management System* lays out a comprehensive management system for aligning the firm's vision of the future with market realities. Based on Hoshin management, the Japanese strategic planning method used by top managers for driving TQM throughout an organization, Lean Management is about deploying vision, strategy, and policy to all levels of daily activity. It is an eminently practical methodology emerging out of the implementation of continuous improvement methods and employee involvement. The key tools of this book build on the knowledge of the worker, multiskilling, and an understanding of the role and responsibilities of the new lean manufacturer.

ISBN 1-56327-085-4 / 182 pages / $65.00 / Order ILMS-B269

Integrated Cost Management
A Companywide Prescription for Higher Profits and Lower Costs
Michiharu Sakurai

To survive and grow, leading-edge companies around the world recognize the need for new management accounting systems suited for today's advanced manufacturing technology. Accountants must become interdisciplinary to cope with increasing cross-functionality, flexibility, and responsiveness. This book provides an analysis of current best practices in management accounting in the U.S. and Japan. It covers critical issues and specific methods related to factory automation and computer integrated manufacturing (CIM), including target costing, overhead management, Activity-Based Management (ABM), and the cost management of software development. Sakurai's brilliant analysis lays the foundation for a more sophisticated understanding of the true value that management accounting holds in every aspect of your company.

ISBN 1-56327-054-4 / 300 pages / $50.00 / Order ICM-B269

Productivity Press, Dept. BK, P.O. Box 13390, Portland, OR 97213-0390
Telephone: 1-800-394-6868   Fax: 1-800-394-6286

Learning Organizations
Developing Cultures for Tomorrow's Workplace
Sarita Chawla and John Renesch, Editors

The ability to learn faster than your competition may be the only sustainable competitive advantage! A learning organization is one where people continually expand their capacity to create results they truly desire, where new and expansive patterns of thinking are nurtured, where collective aspiration is set free, and where people are continually learning how to learn together. This compilation of 34 powerful essays, written by recognized experts worldwide, is rich in concept and theory as well as application and example. An inspiring followup to Peter Senge's groundbreaking bestseller *The Fifth Discipline*, these essays are grouped in four sections that address all aspects of learning organizations: the guiding ideas behind systems thinking; the theories, methods, and processes for creating a learning organization; the infrastructure of the learning model; and arenas of practice.

ISBN 1-56327-110-9 / 575 pages / $35.00 / Order LEARN-B269

New Performance Measures
Brian H. Maskell

Traditional performance measurements are not only ineffective for today's world class organizations, they can actually be harmful—they measure the wrong things. World class companies need measurements that can help them in their quest for improvement. You have to start measuring what your customers really care about such as customer service, quality, and flexibility. Implementing new continuous improvement programs while still using traditional performance measurements will only set you back and give you a lot of useless data. In *New Performance Measures*, you'll learn how to start measuring the things you truly need to know.

ISBN 1-56327-063-3 / 58 pages / $15.95 / Order MS4-B269

Productivity Press, Dept. BK, P.O. Box 13390, Portland, OR 97213-0390
Telephone: 1-800-394-6868   Fax: 1-800-394-6286

Performance Measurement for World Class Manufacturing
A Model for American Companies
Brian H. Maskell

If your company is adopting world class manufacturing techniques, you'll need new methods of performance measurement to control production variables. In practical terms, this book describes the new methods of performance measurement and how they are used in a changing environment. For manufacturing managers as well as cost accountants, it provides a theoretical foundation of these innovative methods supported by extensive practical examples. The book specifically addresses performance measures for delivery, process time, production flexibility, quality, and finance.
ISBN 0-915299-99-2 / 448 pages / $55.00 / Order PERFM-B269

Software and the Agile Manufacturer
Computer Systems and World Class Manufacturing
Brian H. Maskell

The term "agile manufacturing" describes responsive, flexible manufacturing that can deliver better products, faster, at lower cost. This book is the first to address the critical question of how computerization can aid the transition. It shows how computer systems and software designed for individual departments or functions can be adapted to create a world class manufacturing environment that's integrated companywide. Case studies reveal the common characteristics companies have shared in the challenge to computerize and provide guidelines for companies just starting out. This is a nontechnical, practical guide.
ISBN 1-56327-046-3 / 424 pages / $50.00 / Order SOFT-B269

Productivity Press, Dept. BK, P.O. Box 13390, Portland, OR 97213-0390
Telephone: 1-800-394-6868   Fax: 1-800-394-6286

TO ORDER: Write, phone, or fax Productivity Press, Dept. BK, P.O. Box 13390, Portland, OR 97213-0390, phone 1-800-394-6868, fax 1-800-394-6286. Send check or charge to your credit card (American Express, Visa, MasterCard accepted).

U.S. ORDERS: Add $5 shipping for first book, $2 each additional for UPS surface delivery. Add $5 for each AV program containing 1 or 2 tapes; add $12 for each AV program containing 3 or more tapes. We offer attractive quantity discounts for bulk purchases of individual titles; call for more information.

ORDER BY E-MAIL: Order 24 hours a day from anywhere in the world. Use either address:

To order: service@ppress.com

To view the online catalog and/or order: http://www.ppress.com/

QUANTITY DISCOUNTS: For information on quantity discounts, please contact our sales department.

INTERNATIONAL ORDERS: Write, phone, or fax for quote and indicate shipping method desired. For international callers, telephone number is 503-235-0600 and fax number is 503-235-0909. Prepayment in U.S. dollars must accompany your order (checks must be drawn on U.S. banks). When quote is returned with payment, your order will be shipped promptly by the method requested.

NOTE: Prices are in U.S. dollars and are subject to change without notice.